money
and
meaning

To Carol + Micky —
Hope you find
this interesting + informative —

Best Always,

Judy

4/15/08

money
and
meaning

New Ways to Have Conversations about Money with Your Clients—A Guide for Therapists, Coaches, and Other Professionals

Judith Stern Peck

BICENTENNIAL
1807
WILEY
2007
BICENTENNIAL

John Wiley & Sons, Inc.

Library of Congress Cataloging-in-Publication Data

Peck, Judith Stern.
  Money and meaning: new ways to have conversations about money with your clients: a guide for therapists, coaches, and other professionals / by Judith Stern Peck.
    p. cm.
  Includes bibliographical references.
  ISBN 978-0-470-08342-0 (pbk. : alk. paper)
  1. Finance, Personal—Psychological aspects. 2. Money—Psychological aspects. 3. Values.
4. Interpersonal relations—Economic aspects. 5. Personal coaching. I. Title. II. Title: Conversations about money with your clients.
  HG179.P3623 2007
  332.024—dc22

                                               2007028032

Printed in the United States of America

10 9 8 7 6 5 4 3 2 1

My children and their children
Josie, Ben, Maxine, Gabriel, Avery,
Simon, Eliana, Ezra, Oliver, Stephen

. . . Day after day the word goes forth;
    night after night the story is told.

Soundless the speech, voiceless the talk,
    yet the story is echoed throughout the world.

—Psalm 19

Contents

Foreword

A Family Therapist's View of Money and Family Life

When family therapy was in its infancy, a major indictment leveled against this new approach was that it undermined a core tenet of psychotherapy—patient-therapist confidentiality. Many argued that it was the guarantee of confidentiality that helped people talk openly with their therapists about thoughts and actions that they were loath to tell anyone else. Family therapy, so the argument went, violated this rule of confidentiality and therefore could easily do more harm than good when the issues at hand involved the private (and conflicted) fantasies and emotions of people in trouble.

How could it be helpful, the thinking went, for a spouse to talk openly about being disappointed in his or her marriage and family life, or to admit having secret anxieties about work or health issues? Wouldn't it simply just spread the anxiety around and undermine the confidence of children in their parents, or of spouses in one another? Wouldn't it have the potential to stimulate unnecessary rivalries between siblings, or between branches of an extended family? Instead of viewing family conversations as a source for solving dilemmas, families were much more likely to be the *cause* of problems than the *source* of solutions. So the prevailing view of most mental health professionals was to help individuals separate from their families, emotionally if not literally.

Yet the experiences of the pioneers of the family therapy movement led to a very different conclusion. Over and over again, they found that when families had the opportunity to talk openly about their concerns, they left such conversations feeling relief rather than distress. Instead of family members realizing their worst fears—that their ideas would be rejected by other people in the family—quite the opposite occurred. Family members typically would come out of meetings having learned that others in the family *shared* similar concerns or were worrying about the same problems.

A husband who had been holding onto some bad news about an ominous report from his physician (whom he had perhaps consulted without telling his wife), learns that his wife is relieved to hear he has seen a doctor because she has been worried about his health. A child who has been secretly anxious and confused about her mother's depression no longer feels alone.

These dramatic early experiences of family therapists led to two major conclusions: (1) open conversations about individual concerns are a critical initial step toward finding solutions to difficult problems, and (2) reframing problems as shared challenges for families rather than as the responsibility of one family member provides access to creative new possibilities for previously intractable issues. Put another way, family conversations about tough issues, along with willingness to listen to and take advantage of the multiple perspectives that family members bring to the table, can have a transforming effect.

Over the ensuing three decades, family therapy has established itself as a highly effective approach to a wide range of life issues. Mental health problems—depression, substance abuse, childhood behavioral disorders, and the like—are obvious examples. But so, too, are other major life issues such as health crises, job loss, traumatizing events, and family relocations. The same principles that had proved to be a helpful approach to therapy for mental health problems were equally valuable in helping families have problem-focused conversations about other life issues.

A consequence of this expanded view of the potential usefulness of the family therapy approach was a reconceptualization of the role of the family therapist. Rather than being viewed as "therapists" when the issue at hand might be helping a family cope with a chronic medical illness like diabetes or asthma, many mental health professionals preferred thinking of themselves as *family consultants*.

This changing and expanding role could also be seen in the evolution of an institution like the Ackerman Institute for the

Family.[1] Ackerman was founded in 1960 as the first postgraduate family therapy training institute in the United States. Three decades later, although still viewing its core mission as that of training the next generation of leading family therapy practitioners and faculty, the Institute had also expanded its mission to include work in medical center, school, social service, and work environments. In each of these settings, the goal was to bring a family-centered approach to bear on issues relevant to that environment.

Many of these initiatives have proven highly successful. In the work arena, it has turned out that the principles originally developed for family therapy have been useful in helping the members of family-owned businesses wend their ways through the often thorny issues of ownership versus management roles, of intergenerational succession, and of the role of married-in spouses. At the other end of the income spectrum, using family therapy techniques with homeless families who were temporarily living in a shelter setting proved instrumental in helping these families regain a sense of pride and successfully engage in job training programs, find employment, and locate permanent housing.

In fact, the expanding agenda taken on by a place like the Ackerman Institute makes it difficult to think of an important life issue that has not been addressed using a family-relational approach. That is, with one glaring exception—the issue of *money* and family life. As is amply demonstrated in this book, money remains the last great taboo in family life. When we talk here about money as an issue, we are talking about family *attitudes* toward money and family *practices* around money decisions, which are quite different from the concrete discussions that usually occur in families about work concerns. A simple example might be the difference between the practical nuts and bolts of generating money—job satisfaction, employment opportunities, and the like—versus the attitudes and values of the family about money—spending priorities, whether money earned belongs to the family member who generated the income or to the family as a whole, attitudes toward philanthropy,

---

[1]I mention the Ackerman Institute at this point because, as will be detailed later, the Money and Family Life Project which was the central source of data for the ideas to be outlined in this book was developed by Ackerman faculty members under the direction of Judith Stern Peck, and hence formed the larger context for the work of the project team.

where materialism fits in a family's value hierarchy, and what children should be told about a family's financial status.

Parents who seem willing to openly discuss sexual issues with their adolescent children (albeit not always comfortably) avoid at all costs conversations about family wealth or family debt, about seeming inconsistencies in spending priorities, about apparent differences around money issues between the child's own family and that of his or her peers, and about the parents' long-term decisions for the financial well-being of their children.

This reluctance (or perhaps apprehension would be a better word) to have family discussions about money extends to professionals who are ostensibly there to help families make important financial decisions. In part, this is understandable because most financial consultants feel their expertise stems from their knowledge base about a particular area of finance—investments, trusts, estate-planning, and the like. But many a family can tell you a story about how a financial plan that they put in place without understanding the interpersonal relationships within the family led to unforeseen and disastrous consequences.

The thesis of this book is that facilitating conversations within families about money is not only extremely important for the well-being of family members, but also is eminently doable with a clear and cogent framework for carrying out these conversations. The central contention is that the key ingredient is a focus on values. The consultant starts by identifying those core values unique to a particular family and its approach to life, and then examines how those values translate into specific decisions the family makes about important money issues. The framework we advocate to facilitate family conversations about money is first to articulate its core values and how money decisions are either consonant or in conflict with these values, and then to take advantage of the multiple perspectives of different family members in putting these values into action.

Thus *Money and Meaning* explores the myriad ways in which underlying attitudes about money are embedded in family value systems, about how children try to articulate for themselves what these values might be, how perceived inconsistencies between stated values and actual practices lead to intrafamily confusion and conflicts, and how open discussions about continuities around values across generations can help families avoid unnecessary conflicts and misunderstandings that have the potential to tear families apart at times of transition.

Simply to contend that conversations about money are a good thing for families is unfair unless professionals have the tools (road maps) for facilitating such discussions. Without the proper tools, encouraging families to open up about such a potentially emotional topic could easily exacerbate conflict instead of helping families make more satisfying and creative decisions about issues related to money and family life. Thus a major portion of this book is devoted to descriptions of just such tools—process techniques and concrete tasks that we have found facilitate healthy family discussions about money.

In that the Money and Family Life Project evolved within a family therapy research and training institute, it should come as no surprise that many of its principles, techniques, and tools are adaptations of similar ideas that have proved useful in a family therapy setting. But it is also critical to understand that the conversations proposed in this book are *not* to be construed as doing family therapy. They are not to be thought of as useful only for families that are in disarray as a result of conflicts around money. Rather they are broad-based principles that every family consultant should embrace in helping families with specific financial decisions, guiding families in setting up long-range financial plans, or helping families resolve a major conflict that has already arisen because of a disagreement involving money.

PETER STEINGLASS, MD
President Emeritus
Ackerman Institute for the Family

Preface

Talking about Money and Values

People do not like to talk about money. No matter whether the setting is social, familial, or clinical, money remains a taboo subject. This silence is problematic and has detrimental implications for family relationships, whereas the benefits of exploring the subject can be extremely valuable. So why the taboo? And what can we do to change it?

We live in a capitalist society with economics at its center. We struggle to make more and more money, often spending it without much forethought, even impulsively. As a nation, our personal and societal level of debt is greater than it has ever been; yet if and when people do talk about money, the conversation is usually about how they earn it and how they spend it. People tend to avoid entering into other kinds of money conversation because such conversations often lead directly to tension. People do not talk about the meaning of money: what money—having it, earning it, spending it, or giving it away—means to them. For some people, the push to earn can be so overwhelming that it undermines their quality of life. Couples may spend money together without ever talking about how they make their budgeting decisions. Adults may make financial decisions that influence their children without examining that impact. Parents with grown children often have difficulties discussing the issues, and all too often, the children discover financial disarray when they finally get access to their parents' financial matters. If we are not reflectively articulate when making financial decisions, complexities can lie dormant, waiting to confront us.

There is a pervasive inability to have thoughtful conversations within families about financial issues, not because the conversations are insignificant but, on the contrary, because they are so fraught with complex emotional issues. Just scratch the surface, and the issues of shame, fear or guilt often appear. For many of us, money has multiple meanings, some explicit and some implicit, some conscious but most unconscious. These meanings are overdetermined. Some are positive, varying from power and influence to personal security, from freedom to control one's life to the ability to help others. Money can also mean greed, revenge, dependence, ostentation, competition, jealousy, vulnerability, and deception.

What comprises a person's attitude toward money? Where does this attitude come from? How does it affect financial decision making? Family relationships? Professionals seldom make the decision to explore this topic—clinicians, therapists, counselors, and coaches often feel as uncomfortable with it as anyone else. We avoid talking about what it means to us both with our own families and within the clinical space. This might stem from a social taboo related to money talk, or a bias taken from our own family of origin, or merely an idea that money is too mundane a subject and therefore not worthy of our intellectual pursuit.

In tracing the issue of money through generations, it is essential to consider the cultural and relational context. People whose parents lived through the Great Depression remember constant money talk in their homes, but these conversations were often fraught with tension and bickering. As a result, the next generation preferred not to talk about it at all. Whatever the deterrent might be, such avoidance has both practical and emotional implications. Conscious and unconscious attitudes can disrupt communication between family members as well as between professionals and clients, and may prevent the money conversation from flowing easily. Such interference can block the exploration of any linkage to significant collateral issues.

Small wonder, then, that money talk is given short shrift in the clinical space. The subject is an important dimension of life, however, and gives clinicians, coaches, clients, and their families an entry point for unraveling multiple tensions. To begin such a conversation, we must be prepared to sort through the connections in the philosophical, psychological, and practical dimensions of our identity. What do we believe about money? How does it make us feel? What practical impact does it have in our lives? As professionals, we have to become more introspective, more willing to explore these areas within ourselves, before opening up the conversation with our clients. To examine money issues in this way, we need facilitating tools and a frame of reference that provides access to this conversation.

Linking money to values provides the necessary organizing framework for the money conversation. This linkage helps professionals and families break the silence about money, facilitate conversations, and access meanings that can then be transformed, if desired. Linking money and values helps break the taboo and gain access to the underlying issues, thereby creating an expedient method to cut through the overdetermined nature of money. Beginning the money conversation by focusing first on values forms a benign and proud frame of reference for everyone. That linkage can open the door to exploring the conflicts within the family, offering a safe space in which families and couples can have conversations about money with greater understanding.

We each have a system of values that informs all the decisions we make. Daily, we choose how to spend our time as well as our money, using our values as the underlying premises for these decisions. Our values inform our perceptions, actions, and interactions while giving meaning and purpose to our behavior. Yet, we are not always conscious of these meanings. We use this value system as a set of principles that each of us holds in high esteem, reflecting that to which we assign worth. In our behavior, we aspire to use our values to reflect our priorities, and this means that values are not static, but dynamic, changing to fit different situations that arise in our lives. The dynamic nature of values and behavior often becomes the basis for personal growth and development.

This book is an effort to raise this dynamic to consciousness. When we refer to values, we are describing areas of importance as well as qualities of being. These ideals can be personal qualities, such as integrity, faith, or relationships, or they can represent areas that are important to us, such as education, work, or philanthropy. Such values are the standards that inform our behavior, and these deeply felt ideals become the blueprint for how we live our lives.

Where does our system of values originate? How do we acquire our values? Put simply, these ideas and ideals come from our families. As children, we listen to what our parents say, but more importantly, we watch what they do, and so parents, as well as other significant members of a family, become the models from whom we learn these principles. We try to do what they do (or sometimes the opposite) and ultimately internalize the mannerisms and ideals that we observe through our own lens. This adoption of beliefs and values occurs either consciously or unconsciously. In addition, families create rituals and traditions that transmit values, such as celebrations and holidays, athletics, culture, and travel. These activities reinforce the transmission of a family's values, and children learn from all of them. As their world widens, additional outside influences like their school community or their peers affect the internalization process. Values, then, become the underpinning for the development of *human capital*, what was once referred to as "good character." These get transmitted from one generation to the next, as we learn to use values to establish relationships.

Too many of us have lost the consciousness of how our thoughts, feelings, and actions align with our values. The use of values as a frame of reference offers professionals a valid tool for practice. The linkage to money enlarges and enhances the conversation, becoming a way to facilitate exploration.

Acknowledgments

Throughout my adult life, I have consistently explored the meaning of money. I have had multiple conversations with family members, colleagues, clients, and friends. It would be impossible to list all of you who have contributed to the ideas and the application described in this book. Some of you will recognize those journeys in the case vignettes and hopefully appreciate your contribution. Names and circumstances have been changed to protect your privacy. These numerous and varied conversations—both personally and professionally—have informed my thought process. These ideas have been influenced by three dimensions of my life: my family, my Jewish tradition and background, and my professional experience.

For those of you I can name, first and foremost, I want to acknowledge my family. As far back as my adolescent years, my father and I would consistently debate and discuss his "operating" assumption that "economics makes the world go round." Although my mother taught me the skills and mastery of money management, my father was the one who initiated the personal ongoing debate, highlighting the tension between money and relationships. It would not be surprising to most professionals to discover that this dialogue continued with both the father of my children, Leonard, who has his own very clearly defined financial philosophy and my late husband, Stephen, who honored and influenced my journey. My challenge throughout these conversations was my life circumstance, raising my children in the context of wealth. My solution was to focus and impart a value system that expanded beyond materialism. This conversation continues today with my children, Emanuel, Edward, and Andrea, who are raising their children within a similar context in a different era. The family circle has widened to include in-laws, stepchildren, and grandchildren.

The exploration of my Jewish heritage informed the thought process that has led to ideas promoted in this book. In my personal search for meaning, I studied Jewish text and found the wisdom required to tease out the discrepancies that arise quite naturally. This study led me to appreciate the importance of values as a compass. It also taught me about multiple perspectives and contradictions that arise on so many issues. It modeled the management of the discrepancies. I discovered that both the value of values and multiple perspectives, are applicable universally and have been part of an ongoing dialogue for thousands of years.

Using this multifaceted lens that combined my family therapy background, my Jewish studies, and my life experience, led me to appreciate the inherent complexities of this question of money and meaning. All of the above led me to explore the premise of a values linkage to money. I tested out my ideas in the clinical space and with my professional colleagues.

I want to acknowledge my professional colleagues who have participated in these discussions, especially the team members of the Money and Family Life Project at the Ackerman Institute for the Family. I would like to thank Dr. Peter Steinglass for giving me the opportunity to form the project team and then become a member. In addition, the others that joined initially and who took a leap of faith and struggled through the beginning stage of defining our work. They are: Scott Budge, Susan Burden, Marcia Sheinberg, and Sally Wigutow. Elizabeth Bailey, Shira Ronen, and Greg Rogers have since joined the group and have contributed to furthering these ideas through practice and conversation. We have all used the methodology personally and professionally and so I would like to acknowledge those clients I have known, as well as those my colleagues have known, and express my gratitude for your input through these various channels of communication. Lois Braverman, our new president at the Institute has been a continuing support and resource for our work.

Every project requires the invested perspective of an Advisory Group. We formed that group in the early years of our project. I want to thank all of you for your feedback on our work, Melissa Berman, President of Rockefeller Philanthropy Advisers, Iva Kaufman, Family Philanthropy Initiative at UJC, Richard Lavin at Tiger 21, Stephen Shulman at Anchin, Bloch & Anchin, Michael Smith at US Trust, and Heidi Steiger.

I am also deeply grateful to my friends who have been engaged in this conversation for a long time and even took the time to review initial drafts of this book: Sharon Strassfeld, Ronit Dolev, and Kathryn Steinberg. A special thanks to Charles Bronfman and his late wife Andrea who agreed to participate in the first seminar on money and family life five years ago. And to colleagues who have given me guidance, support, and challenge in this process: Byron Wien, Dr. Ron Toffel, Dr. Harold Koplowitz, Jay Hughes, and Paul Schervisch. I am indebted to all of you for the points of wisdom you conveyed whenever and wherever we had conversations.

Finally, the people who both motivated me and supported me in the actual writing of this book. First, I would like to thank Michael J. McGandy, who recruited me and helped me develop a book proposal when I hardly knew I had the content for it. A big thank you to Elisheva Urbas who helped me take that proposal and develop the contents for this book, keeping me focused and clear in that pursuit and lastly, Peggy Alexander and her staff at Wiley, who helped see the text to completion through its many iterations.

money
and
meaning

Introduction

The Money and Family Life Project at the Ackerman Institute

The ideas promoted in this book were generated by the dynamic research of the Money and Family Life project team at the Ackerman Institute for the Family, which I head. The complex landscape of money and families has multiple dimensions and requires reflection through myriad lenses. Our study focused on exploring money in a relational context. To do this, we took into consideration work that had been done over a long time in many different contexts, incorporating ideas from family systems theory and family business writings, as well as other academic and non-academic writings and presentations. The approach developed by the faculty of the Ackerman Institute, under the leadership of Marcia Sheinberg, Director of Training, has informed our methodology.

The project team's process evolved organically, with ideas and tools emerging from group discussions, interactive seminars, and case consultations. We continue to refine these during the ongoing process of applying the methodology. The application of these methods has proven to be successful in multiple ways for professionals who work with families and seek enhancement of the money dialogue.

The historical perspective of our study encompasses written material as well as information that has been covered in specific lectures and presentations. Over the past 20 years, many colleagues interested in this work have migrated to the family business arena, finding it an accessible way to address money matters and family systems issues. Most of the family business/family wealth literature deals with how families manage their financial assets. Therefore, although the literature on money in general is vast, there are few clinical or academic works about money and families. In the family systems literature, the only book written specifically on money and the family is Cloe Madanes's book, *The Secret Meaning of Money*, written in 1994. Madanes addresses the secrecy of money, the covert struggles within relationships, and the ultimate power dynamics manifest in couples and families.

Jay Hughes, a lawyer and family wealth consultant, has written about the need for developing "human capital" a term used to highlight individuals and their strengths within the family, "alongside social, intellectual and financial capital." He describes what that might encompass and challenges the complexity faced by families with wealth. He focuses on the potential strength of individuals and the meaning that could have for the collective as the family moves generationally.

The late Scott Fithian developed a paradigm for the application of a values-based approach to financial planning and promoted a questionnaire of values to highlight the connection. Paul G. Schervish, Professor of Sociology and Director of the Center on Wealth and Philanthropy at Boston College, studied the subjects of money, wealth, and philanthropy. In his lectures, Schervish advocates the education toward values and morals as a spiritual companion to material inheritance. He argues that providing a moral compass will enable people to make more discerning choices around money. As our team explored the linkage of money and values, our thinking was shaped by professionals like Hughes, Fithian, and Schervish.

Methodology

Our challenge was to develop a methodology to break the taboo of money talk in families. We understood that silence creates obfuscation and dysfunction in families, and sought ways to move beyond silence, secrecy, and power into meaning-based exploration of family dynamics. Our agenda was to learn how to get our clients to talk about money in their relational context.

Based at the Ackerman Institute, our project integrated two methodological approaches, the Ackerman approach and the perspective of those who had worked in the family business arena. Our alignment with the training approach at the Institute became an important focus. The perspective of the family business arena widened the scope of our knowledge and our process, and so our project's methodology was influenced by both paradigms.

To ensure that multiple perspectives were represented, we began the project by forming an interdisciplinary team. Each member of the group represented a different voice, field of discipline, age, or gender. The initial interdisciplinary group comprised six people: two members in leadership positions at the Institute, a family business consultant with expertise in organizational development, a psychologist who had changed careers and gone into the financial services world, a family therapist who had dealt with financial and estate matters in her own remarried family, and myself, a family therapist and family business consultant. Later on, three more members joined the team: a family therapist who had been a financial writer, a business consultant who was interested in the psychology of money, and an investment and family advisor turned family systems thinker. Their names in order of description: Dr. Peter Steinglass, Marcia Sheinberg, Sally Wigutow, Scott Budge, Susan Burden, Elizabeth Bailey, Shira Ronen, and Greg Rogers.

The differences in our professional and personal backgrounds created multiple obstacles for us to overcome. The variances between the stance of therapist and that of consultant surfaced regularly. Members of the Ackerman Institute were steeped in the relational approach to family therapy. The others, who were more focused on a family/business model, brought forward ideas about how to work with multiple competing systems when roles overlap, when clear boundaries do not exist, and when alignment between talk and action is often missing. Those of us who had worked with family businesses understood the challenge of working with multiple systems, where the issues are complex and entangled. Those of us from the family therapy world understood the tension between gathering data and a more process-oriented exploration. The integration of influences from these multiple perspectives was challenging, often reminiscent of a multigenerational family group.

The initial stage of our group dynamic reflected the thesis of this book: money was a taboo subject even for us. We were reluctant to explore the subject of money within our group as well as in our specific practices. The gaps among us in this area were great. The initial group process was frustrating, requiring multiple conversations with individual members before we found the issue that could unite us for our project's work. Eventually, we came to the linkage of money and values as an organizing frame. This linkage reduced the reluctance and resistance in our own group process and opened up our discussions around money. Our own process thus informed our sense of what would be helpful to others. We had become part of our own learning laboratory. These internal discussions were effectively the first stage of our action research and helped in turn to define the next phase of our work.

Applications

Having clarified our own understanding, we quickly expanded outward to test our emerging ideas at workshops and seminars, partnering with various organizations to facilitate these conversations. Initially, these were organizations that provided financial services to families and held conferences for those families to explore money and relational issues. In addition, we invited actual families to participate in seminars at the Institute. We started with families of wealth, because this constituency, with so many unanswered questions about their families and money, had particular difficulty with money talk.

There was little resistance to our outreach as we were a neutral party whose clear mission related to the health of the family. We actually became a welcome convener for many families dealing with money issues, particularly because we were not selling them a service or product. We were seen as providing a safe space where family members could talk to each other and with others who were grappling with similar issues. We ran multiple seminars and workshops for this population, testing methods that incorporated the Ackerman approach and the specific tools of our project.

At the same time, we developed workshops for professionals working with these families. The response to the seminars and workshops was positive. We used the feedback to inform our thinking, which in turn influenced our next round of presentations. We refined our focus to "money and marriage" and "money and children." With our focus on money and children, we conducted workshops with parents in schools, expanding our reach in terms of social class. We used these same tools with families in our practices. We formed an advisory group of professionals from the various institutions with whom we were collaborating, and this group provided helpful feedback. In addition, we had case consultations within the group, using values as the basis for discussion. This recursive process with the varying constituencies defined our qualitative research.

The Family Unit

Central to the Ackerman approach is the view of the family as the unit of analysis, where multiple perspectives form a challenging environment. Each member of a family has a specific view of an issue and brings a unique meaning to that understanding. "The concept of systemic thinking centers on how families within and across generations construct these meanings and how these meanings inform family interaction and constrain the flexibility and capacity for change among family members."

This concept of the family as a complex system is particularly relevant to the exploration of money and family life. Social class, culture, race, and gender are multiple levels of context that add complexity to all family systems, but that come to bear in especially complicated ways around issues of money. Traversing the complexity with a focus on changing relationships or relational behavior became the challenge within which we addressed the taboo of money.

Facilitating Conversations about Money

To explore any topic as complex as money in the relational context poses several tasks for the clinician or coach even before beginning the conversation. Given the history in the field, our position at the Institute, and our own group process, three elements became significant for us: the safety of the context, the neutrality of the language, and the facilitation of process while addressing content.

We identified these as the tasks required for the backdrop of the conversation, but understood that the professional's self-understanding in this area is key as well.

The first task then became the attention to an environment where everyone could feel secure in the conversation. By creating a safe space through structured conversation, collaborative stance, and reflective dialogue, the professional can lay the foundation for facilitating the conversation and breaking the taboo.

For many families, practical and relational connections are entangled, and conversations around money and values create emotional and attitudinal resonances, unleashing past meanings and creating new tensions and conflicts. Families and couples need a safe entry point, where the language used can diminish the confusion around money. When a structured conversation occurs using a common language, the professional can access these premises and use the common, safe language to neutralize the emotional reactivity. A values construct can become the groundwork for change, whereby clarity and meaning become elements leading to a more constructive conversation. Relationships can shift to a better balance and assumptions about the other are less likely to lead to unwarranted reactions.

Linking money to values provides this common language for structured conversation. Because money is such an "overdetermined" subject, giving people a nonjudgmental language with which to talk about it provides a safe environment. Talking about values is easy, and so assigning values to financial decisions as a second step comes naturally. Giving clients permission to expose discrepancies, furthermore, expands the conversation safely. Thus, promoting the connection of money talk to values serves a practical purpose, creating a benign and positive frame of reference for everyone to tell their narrative and confront their discrepancies between thought, feelings, and action.

For the facilitator, the collaborative stance is key. Joining the family or client as a fellow explorer of the issues rather than as the "expert" enhances the quality of the environment, allowing clients to feel respected and acknowledged. Determining the common agenda in the relational context can be significant, offering the contradiction for individuals and making them more conscious of the tension between individual and collective agendas. The professional can query meaning, acknowledge feeling, and define the issues. These techniques compel the family to address the distinctions and meanings that inform their behavior.

When assuming a collaborative stance, the clinician needs to be cognizant of the pacing and sequencing of questions, taking the cue from the client's responses. The skill and art of timing is imperative in enhancing the facilitation process. As a professional, it is important not to get too far ahead of clients in thought and outcome. The art is to collaborate with clients as they move into greater consciousness of the issues, to listen and use the feedback to inform the next query, exploring meaning.

In facilitating the process, it is often expedient to reference the connection between the content of the conversation and the ongoing process. This may guide the client to greater understanding of the emotional connections to the subject that have previously been subtext. Enhanced awareness of their process empowers the family.

These tasks—creating safe context, using a collaborative stance, paying attention to pacing and sequencing, and connecting the content and process—become the primary focus for the professional in facilitating the money conversation. When one creates this context and then links values to money as an organizing frame for the money-focused conversation, the taboo dissolves and a more productive conversation surfaces, opening a more transparent dialogue within the family.

Operating Principles and Process

During our workshops and seminars with families and professionals, they frequently ask us for solutions to problems ("What should we do when . . . ?"). In our team discussions, we were clear about our position on these questions. We were promoting a change of process for people, not a particular set of solutions. Rather than offering concrete solutions, we promoted a values-based approach that could constantly be revisited and fine-tuned. This reluctance to present specific answers led us to identify the defined objective of the work: *to change the process used to talk and think about money in a relational context.* This would require motivation on the clients' part, and an understanding of the impact for them and their relationships. If we presented these principles to them, this might influence their motivation to change. Our ability to convey this line of thinking became our challenge. We eventually refined three basic operating principles and then defined specific recommendations, creating a process that was transformative rather than transactional:

The Principles

1. We live using values as our map and guide, but are not always aware of these values. When we become aware of them, we can use them to better inform our behavior and decisions.
2. The greater the discrepancy between values espoused by a family and the behavior toward money within family life, the more problematic the family interaction around money.
3. Discrepancies focus attention and bring issues to center stage. Clarity about our values, and around the discrepancies between values and behavior among family members, creates a stronger, healthier-functioning family life.

To give people recommendations based on these principles, we came up with the following five points:

1. *Agree to disagree.* Recognize and acknowledge differences within the family unit.
2. *Appreciate the complexity.* Embrace multiple perspectives, and push for discovery of the essence of the issue.
3. *Walk the talk.* Be aware of normal contradictions and discrepancies between talk and action both interpersonally and intrapersonally.
4. *Use a developmental perspective.* Choose age-appropriate vehicles to transmit the value.
5. *Understand distinctions.* Consider distinctions when solving a problem or managing a dilemma.

Although these appear to be relatively simple ideas, the difficulty is in the consciousness and consistency of their application. We seek to help our clients have constructive conversations about money in a relational context. The following three steps lead to this changed process:

1. Identification of and awareness of values
2. Application and clarity of communication using values
3. Transformation of values (when chosen)

When working with families and money, each of the preceding steps can stand alone. The completion of all three steps depends on the client's desire to integrate or internalize this process. Through our project's work, we have applied this methodology in short presentations, daylong workshops, short-term groups, clinical/coaching sessions, and ongoing treatment. We consistently found that using a values-based approach to money talk in families creates positive results.

Identifying one's values is the first step in our paradigm. We all use values to inform our decision making, although we are not always conscious of what those implicit values are and how they affect our decisions. In becoming more attentive to our thought process, we can reduce tension both individually and interpersonally. When we reflect on our values and their alignment with action, we can begin to understand the tensions that creep into our daily lives, causing stress and discomfort. Awareness stimulates reflective thought.

In applying reflective thought to our values, we experience the consistencies and inconsistencies simultaneously. Sometimes we focus on our idealized values; at other times we investigate the actual pattern of values as reflected in our behavior. There might be contradictions between what we say and what we do. In defining the myriad ways in which these discrepancies occur, we understand how many confusing and mixed messages we send to others. The use of values as an organizing frame brings clarity to this communication. Even when there are discrepancies, it becomes a less complicated message to send and receive if we explain the contradiction. It imposes a consistent meaning to our communication both interpersonally and individually.

Transformation can take place in two ways, either around a particular issue or through the internalization of a new approach to thinking about money talk. The motivation for change is necessary for either process to occur. The change is reflected in thought, behavior, and attitude, either specific or more global. If someone has historically believed that work, as a value, means only work at a job for pay, but now expands the meaning of this value to include the results of efforts or activities requiring skill and knowledge (not always linked to pay), then the person has transformed the idea and it may be relevant to a new set of circumstances. This is a change in thought about a particular issue. When a values-based approach becomes the format for all financial decision making and communication, change takes place both internally and interpersonally. This would happen over a longer period and would encourage better familial relationships.

How to Use This Book

The book is divided into two parts. Part One has two chapters. The first chapter describes the tools that link money and values and explains how to use them. The second chapter explores the clinician's experience, processes, and the implementation of the methodology in the clinical space. Professionals who are not comfortable with the subject and want to use these tools need to explore their own values and their linkage to money.

Part Two applies the methodology to multiple family situations. Chapter 3 applies this thinking to couples by using vignettes from case studies for description and application of these tools. Chapters 4 and 5 address money and children, using case studies of families with children of various ages and focusing on the integration of the tools and operating principles. Chapter 6 addresses the single adult years. Finally, Chapter 7 looks at various family configurations around money and life transitions such as death, divorce, and chronic illness. These are often difficult times in family life, and money is all too often a major issue and challenge.

The methodology described here is new and innovative in breaking the taboo of money talk. This pathbreaking work opens up channels of communication that have not been accessible to families, and we are confident that this methodology will enhance family functioning in a positive direction. Promoting values as a frame of reference for decision making and reflective thought can vastly improve the family and social context.

PART 1

The Professional's Toolbox

Chapter 1

Tools for Talking about Money and Values

To work with our clients, the project team at Ackerman developed a three-part methodology to break the money taboo and enable the conversation. In Stage 1, we help make the person's value system explicit by raising those values into consciousness and clarifying them. This awareness provides a framework for the linkage of values to money, paving the way to Stage 2. In this stage, we apply the now explicit values to financial decisions and then identify and specifically address the inherent contradictions in the client's life. This clarification affords easier access to the emotions attached to the situation that are significant, if unexpressed, elements in the conversation. Finally, in Stage 3, it is possible to *transform* the client's values around money, if desired. In this chapter, we discuss three tools the therapist can use to bring a client's value system to awareness, help the client apply those values in financial decisions, and create an environment for change. These include two card sorts and a money focused genogram.

When people acquire the tools for conversations about money, they are more apt to make those discussions productive and supportive of their relationships. When used with skill and understanding, these tools trigger reflective thought and empower clients to apply this new thought process to financial decision making as well as to general decision making. They provide the language for talking about discrepancies and help begin the conversation and process of behavior change. This safer context improves the potential for sorting out the anxieties that may accompany these conversations. It brings issues and motivations into sharper focus and gives access to tension points—power and powerlessness, shame and pride, fear or guilt—all meanings that have historically been connected to money. The challenge is to discern the connection to the money topic that is laden with these multiple meanings.

Card Sort Technique

Instead of an abstract values discussion, we use a concrete method in our workshops, seminars, and private client work. After considering various options, we found that using a *card sort* technique was particularly effective because it provides clear descriptions as well as a way to prioritize and make distinctions. Moreover, because of its concreteness, the card sort tool evokes reflective and applicable understanding of values.

We use two sets of cards—one represents *content values* and the other represents *process values*—and we encourage users to sort both sets into the order that reflects their value priorities.

Content Values Card Sort. The content values cards name both qualities of being and areas of importance, such as *education, work, philanthropy, relationships, material possessions, spirituality, financial responsibility, physical needs, personal values, public service, recreation, economics, work,* and *ethical values* (see Appendix I). One of these values is printed on the top of each card. Under each heading, bullet points stimulate the thought process toward the meaning of these values. Under the heading "Ethical Values," we have listed "Integrity," "Justice," and "Fairness." The bullet points elucidate each value, a further distinguishing catalyst that moves the individual's process constructively and expediently. They also trigger associative meanings.

Thus, the first step in the card sort is simply to help people feel comfortable with the cards and the activity of sorting them. As such, we were not intent on creating the perfect set of cards or the only possible set of cards. Our objective, whether in a group setting or a workshop, was to get the participants to enter the conversation, which would enable them to begin to grapple with the issues for themselves. Individuals in the group were encouraged to talk about their choices, and most people enjoyed the exercise because it gave them a safe structure for the conversation. To promote the importance of listening to each other, we asked families to abstain from commenting while another family member was talking.

Case Study: Jim and Gail Finally Talk about Money

During their 15 years of marriage, Gail and Jim have never been able to speak about money. Now, however, Gail can no longer manage their budget without Jim's participation. Moreover, they are reaching a juncture in their lives where they will have to make important quality-of-life decisions. Their marriage feels strong to them overall, but they need to talk about their financial situation.

Our goal for Gail and Jim is to help them find ways to talk productively about money and their financial situation. Enabling them to make their values explicit will help the conversation about money become productive and supportive of their overall relationship. Although some clinical situations might call for abstract discussions to assist clients in illuminating their values, in conversations about money, it is far simpler and more productive to use a concrete approach.

Handing a set of content values cards to both Jim and Gail, I asked them first to look at the cards and become familiar with them. Next, I directed them to sort the cards into two piles (with no set number in either pile), creating categories of "an important value" and "not an important value." Gail's initial response was, "These are all important to me," followed by, "This is more difficult than I thought it would be." Acknowledging the difficulty in discriminating, I encouraged them to proceed, noting that creating the priorities was actually our objective. The second step of this exercise was to narrow the important value choices down to the top four.

This second step can be challenging. The objective is to identify core values and distinguish between core values and situational values. Core values are those premises that inform a person's behavior whether at work, at home, or with friends. No matter which one of our multiple identities we are inhabiting—be it colleague, spouse, parent, child, friend, or sibling—these values consistently define each of us. These are the basic values that inform who we are, what we think, how we perceive ourselves, and how we act. Sometimes we refer to the core values as our *internal landscape,* at other times as a *moral compass*. Historically, we would be referring to character when alluding to these values, which might also be described as the idealized version of the self.

By contrast, situational values are more fluid values. These values can change depending on a specific time of life. A person approaching retirement might assign value to cultural, philanthropic, and recreational opportunities, whereas physical or economic values might have predominated at an earlier stage of life. This concept of situational values as distinct from core values highlights the fluidity of values development. During our seminars and workshops, we convey the idea that depending on our stage of life, certain situational ideals and ideas will become more important than others. The consciousness of this fluidity brings people to the essence of themselves, supporting a positive dimension of personal agency.

Jim and Gail both had difficulty with this part of the exercise. They kept looking at the two piles before them, trying repeatedly to choose their top four. Gail kept reshuffling her cards and looking up at Jim. I told them that the exercise was designed to be done separately by each person and that later we would talk together about the outcome. I reiterated that there were no specific "right" answers and that the objective was to provide a framework for greater self-knowledge and a safe context for discussing different perspectives.

When Gail and Jim finished, I started the conversation by asking Gail to tell us the values she had chosen. The four cards she chose were "relationships," "spirituality," "financial responsibility," and "ethical values." She talked about the tension she had experienced while choosing her four core values, but noted how comfortable she felt with her final decisions. She walked us through her thought process and explained how she had made her decision. There were conflicts for her between public service and ethical values, but she reasoned that ethics for her was the overriding value, and public service seemed like a natural outcome of having strong ethical values. I turned to Jim and asked if he would have chosen these values to describe Gail. He said most definitely. The only one he would have been hesitant to assign to her was the spiritual one. He had difficulty in recognizing this as a value, but he understood Gail's commitment to it.

Doing this card sort with families and couples presents the opportunity, as it did with Gail and Jim, for a relational focus and the exploration of individual and interpersonal dimensions. The card sort becomes a pathway to addressing the similarities among and differences between family members in a safe environment with a structured conscious dialogue. The values clarification exercise raises awareness and organizes these values as guidelines for behavior, introducing multiple perspectives and acknowledging differences. It affords the clinician or coach the opportunity to examine with clients those perspectives and the meanings behind them, as well as to explore the relational aspects by asking how each would describe the other using the card sort. Whether spouses are present, or the group is intergenerational, the same questions are used. With an intergenerational group, the card sort technique allows reflection on the transmission of values, creating a positive context for family conversations.

In describing his choices, Jim started with "relationships," noting that Gail's commitment to him and his desire to be there for her had been a core value for him. He described her as his best friend and assumed she felt the same. He also noted how the "work" value card had triggered tension for him. When I asked what he meant, he talked about the experience of losing his job 10 years earlier. Having lost a substantial income, he had been unable to talk to Gail about it. He was ashamed of having been fired, and worried that talking to her about his sense of shame would give her "arrows for her quiver."

Jim's response to the first step of the card sort was poignant, enlightening, and productive. Citing his strong commitment to the relationship enhanced the already present bond between this couple. His openness and honesty about the work issue surprised Gail. They had never had this conversation, and because the work issue was so related to their financial circumstances, it became significant for our work together. We had not yet linked values to money, but Jim seemed to take his leap in this first step of the card sort. The most noteworthy outcome in this step of the exercise was that each person stated separately a commitment to the relationship as a core value. Highlighting this was significant, especially for Gail, because it neutralized her reactivity to the financial dimension of their marriage and allowed her to be present to hear Jim talk about his shame.

The next step in the card sort is to have the participants reshuffle the cards and think about their most recent serious financial decision. Such decisions include financing a home, developing an annual budget, deciding to send a child to private school, or planning a family vacation. After coming up with a specific financial decision, clients use the card sort to choose the four values that informed it. Having just done the card sort with a focus on self, they now have an opportunity to see whether there is alignment or discrepancy between the values they chose for an application exercise and the chosen values in the first set.

This second exercise presents the concept of contradiction. Inevitably, there is not an exact alignment between the personal values in the first exercise and those in the second that inform financial decision making. The key concept is to raise awareness by highlighting the tension between what we think and say and what we do. While discrepancies are both natural and normal, the objective here is to give people a way to talk about them.

Now we were ready for the next step, in which each person takes the 14 cards and, having identified their particular financial decision, sorts the cards into more and less important values relative to that issue. Then the participant chooses the top four values from the "most important" pile of cards, with the focus on the four values that informed the financial decision.

Jim and Gail decided to focus on their budget as their most important financial issue. In anticipation of the next phase of our work, I asked each of them to prepare a separate list of their assets and liabilities, and a projected budget. Then we returned to the card sort. They both reshuffled their cards and began by making two piles and then refined their most important pile. Jim offered to go first this time. He started out by highlighting the facts of their budget decision. His discomfort with the topic was reflected in his detached presentation. Jim attempted to give a businesslike statement, but he had difficulty identifying the values he would or could use to inform their annual budget. With hesitation, he cited "economics," "work," "education," and "ethical" values. Jim ascribed these values to the future and said that he would now apply them to their budget decisions. Curiously, he did not want to think about the values that had informed past decisions—those memories were too painful. Thus, without ever intending to do so, Jim addressed the issues that Gail had raised in our first meeting: the lack of coordination of effort and the absence of a business partnership in their marriage.

As Jim began to talk openly about the discrepancy between what he would like to earn and the salary he could actually achieve, his shame was palpable. He had never before addressed what had happened when his income was drastically reduced 10 years earlier; it was a conversation he had determinedly avoided. During that difficult financial time, he had even used Gail's credit card to pay some of his personal obligations from his first marriage, which had infuriated Gail. Now, she was hearing the other side of the story. Gail's reaction to Jim's story was both compassionate and skeptical. The positive dimension for her, she explained, was that they were actually beginning the conversation, something they had been unable to do for a long, long time.

Making the discrepancies explicit and acknowledging their normalcy moved the conversation dramatically. The sequencing of these card sort exercises paced the process. Thus, Jim's ability to communicate the motivations for the inconsistencies he detected brought to the foreground the dimensions for dialogue with new meanings. Talking about the discrepancies between thought, talk, and action allowed the professional dealing with financial matters to foster the link between money and values—even with all the contradictions.

The Process Values Card Sort

The sequencing in sorting the content values cards helps clients identify individual values, reflect on how those values inform their decision making, and recognize the inherent contradictions that might be embedded between decisions and actions. Emphasizing these three objectives enhances and illuminates the conversation with clients. They walk away with specific tools to use when talking about money. They have gained the ability to consciously change and transform their behavior.

The second card sort addresses *process values*, a newer and more difficult concept for some people. This card sort relates to how we make decisions, rather than why. We ascribe these values to the processes used for making decisions as well as implementing them. Again, this sort raises awareness and opens productive conversation.

The nine values in the second set of cards specify process values, the *how* of financial decisions (and indeed of decision making in general). The nine values in our deck of process cards are *reflective thinking, collaboration, hierarchy, inclusive values, exclusive values, dialogue, transparency, empowerment,* and *equality* (see Appendix II for these cards). The goal is to raise awareness of a course of action (process), and to create a safe environment for pursuing conversations. These concepts are new for many users, and they may be much more fluid than the content values. The process values that guide people vary depending on the life circumstances and the ages of the participants. Family cultures, too, are reflected in the choices people make.

Case Study: Charles Changes His Decision Making

Charles had been managing his business affairs for some time and wanted to bring his grown children into the firm. There had been a rift between Charles and his children years ago, and consequently they were skeptical about trying to work together. A key issue became how business decisions were to be made, since the sons' bad experience with their father had been in exactly this area. Accordingly, we scheduled a family meeting to discuss decision making. At that meeting, I used the process values card sort as an entry into our discussion.

Charles used this set of cards as prompters to identify his choices and the embedded contradiction for him. He identified the three cards that were important to him, "collaboration," "transparency," and "empowerment." He quickly identified the discrepancy inherent in his choice of collaboration. Although he very much wanted to include his sons and collaborate with them, his natural mode was quite the opposite. He was an only child and had always made his own decisions, accessing resources and employing advisors, but never conferring with others about his actual decisions. The cards helped him identify the potential discrepancy, and he asked his sons to flag him when they saw this happening. He understood that this old behavior would sabotage his new objective to create a collaborative model of decision making for his business affairs.

These discrepancies seem to be particularly significant in an intergenerational context. If a parent says one thing and acts in a contradictory manner, the children, no matter what age, find that inconsistency difficult to comprehend and are confused by the mixed messages. Frequently, it is the failure to acknowledge and define these inevitable discrepancies that becomes the crucial issue. The lack of communication about discrepancies between parents and children (or siblings or spouses) has a negative impact that leads to interpersonal tensions. The card sort can make the conflict explicit and provide the language with which to explore it. Clients can then communicate the meaning of their behavior, acknowledge the tensions, and ultimately make changes, if they desire to do so. It also opens the door for actual collaboration if and when a client gives others permission to flag the discrepant behavior pattern as it surfaces.

Because Charles could identify and flag his discrepancy with the card sort, his sons began to trust the invitation to join him. This was an important step in reaching his objective because it reduced the tension and provided a path for aligning his objective and actions. Charles used the card sort to get to the fundamental value and meaning for him, which allowed him to communicate openly with his family. They all understood that the old pattern, where Charles would make a decision without including anyone, might continue. At the same time, they were given the green light to talk about this with Charles when it occurred, and he committed to being open to the discussion. This conversation provided a new meaning to the behavior, and became the first manifestation of the collaborative process that Charles had identified as his objective.

When this kind of change occurs, the motivation for the transformation becomes accessible and conscious. Charles had been an only child who had been a solo decision maker for most of his life, but his father had never introduced him into the family finances. On his father's death, Charles, who had no understanding of the financial world, was thrust into managing substantial assets without any apprenticeship or understanding. He was determined that this would not happen to his sons. Although Charles's family had believed in passing on the assets, there had been no educational process or preparation for stewardship, and Charles had been left adrift as a result. He wanted to integrate his sons into the family's financial decision-making process during his lifetime. Charles hoped to retain a value he had learned from his family of origin and yet transform that value into one that would foster better interfamilial relationships. Because he was so aware of wanting to hand down the family assets differently, the transformation process for him could be transparent and effective.

The process values cards can be used to highlight the transfer and transformation of values between generations. There are three steps to this technique. The first task focuses on choosing those values that describe the decision-making process in one's family of origin. In the second step, clients sort the cards according to the ways they envision processing decisions within the family. The third and final step is to apply the card sort to a specific financial event. In debriefing this exercise, the discrepancy usually unfolds in two ways. The more flagrant contradiction is between the family of origin and nuclear family processes. Inherently, the impulse between generations is to do things differently and better in the newer generation, and so merely acknowledging the difference or similarity is important. The second dimension of contradiction might be more subtle, as it surfaces between the idealized and actual version of the decision-making process. This card sort set and exercise is a good tool for introducing clients to the concept of process, which is becoming more and more identified in working with complex family situations.

If Charles had done the card sort in these three steps, he would have noted first that in his family of origin, decisions were made hierarchically and exclusively. His father never talked to him about any financial matters, nor did he include him in any decision making. In the second step, Charles might have chosen "transparency" and "collaboration" as his ideal process values. The third step would then bring to light the discrepancy for Charles, prompting him to address the ways he makes financial decisions and the hurdle that would surface with his desire to include his sons in those decisions.

This card sort can highlight the potential for change. In Charles's case, the value of legacy transfer is maintained. The transformation that Charles wants to make is in the process or "how to" dimension. Creating the linkage to values with the card sort is an expedient and illuminating technique here because it underscores the ambivalence that underlies undefined tensions.

In making financial decisions, professional advisors often seek to complete the transaction. When nothing happens, they wonder why. In our work, we have learned to look at both the what and the how of financial transactions. These decisions are inherently complex. The values card sort clarifies the multiple dimensions of such transactions.

The Focused Genogram

A work- and money-focused genogram is another methodology to develop a client's understanding. The genogram is a tool that has been used in the family therapy field for many years. It is a graphic chart or emotional map of a family, describing membership and relationships. It highlights themes throughout a family's history as well as the time line of significant events within the family's life cycle, such as births, deaths, divorces, and the onset of disease. Together, professionals and clients explore family relationships and the repercussions and influences permeating generational transmission. This provides clients with a graphic portrayal of the family dynamics that have informed their lives, focusing on the areas of money and work. This exercise often leads to the motivation to change. Monica McGoldrick, an expert in the field of family therapy, has written extensively on the use of genograms.

In doing a focused genogram, we make the immediate membership of the family clear and then ask questions that relate to the meaning of money and the ways it was managed in the relational context. Thus, the genogram traces the data of the family as well as its emotional processes. Our team developed the following specific questions to help delineate the messages and attitudes about money

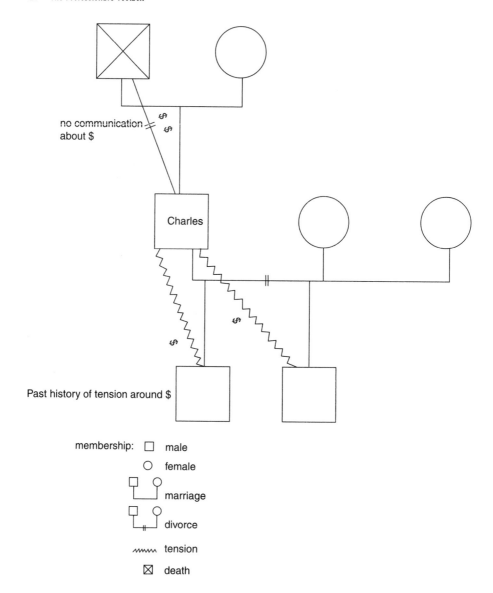

and work in the family. They focus on the relational dimension of money and work and move from the past to the present, with an emphasis on the interpersonal connections and the patterns that have evolved:

Questions for Exploring the Past

- What was your family's attitude toward money when you were growing up? Did they talk about it? Argue about it? Did they talk with you or your siblings directly about money? If so, when and how?

- What did your parents teach you about money? Did you receive different messages from each of them?
- Growing up, what was your understanding of your family's financial status, and how was that communicated to you?
- How old were you when you had your first job?
- Did your parents contribute to your education? Did they give you money, or lend you money, after you left home?
- How easy was it for you to get money from your parents for the following: education, clothing, books, music, vacation, charitable contributions?

Questions for Exploring the Present and Future

- Do you have any fears about money? Did your parents? Are these fears related to any actual experiences around money?
- When did you realize that you might be reenacting the behaviors around money from your family of origin? Did you then choose to replicate or transform them?
- Do you talk with your children about money? Do they have an easier time than you did asking for toys, clothing, books, or charitable contributions?

Answering these questions sharpens the client's awareness of powerful relationships and the experiences of shame or fear associated with them. In probing for the meaning of money within the family system, the emotional component and the connection between present and past will surface. When this happens, the conversation takes a different turn and the connections between money and fears, money and power, or money and shame reveal themselves. Often the "aha" moment occurs here, and the work continues by tracing the particular issue with its emotional connection throughout the client's life journey, reaffirming that the issue and the connected affect have set a pattern relating to money. The art in using this tool is to deepen the client's understanding of how the family's past emotional process influences today's attitudes and patterns.

In subsequent conversations with Charles, I decided to use the focused genogram to enhance his resolve to transform his decision making. The consciousness of his desired change, coupled with an ongoing understanding of how he formulated his original decision-making process, would serve him throughout the anticipated transformation. Charles observed while I constructed the genogram. The visual and interactive process stimulated his thought process. He could appreciate the emotional overlay for his father around work and money. He refreshed his understanding of how this affected his parents' relationship. Charles could then begin to appreciate that what had happened in his first marriage was a result of the way he had handled money and work. This connection was crucial as he considered his relationship with his sons. This reflection gave Charles an emotional connection to his behavior, reinforcing his motivation to change his patterns and launching him into the trajectory to transformation.

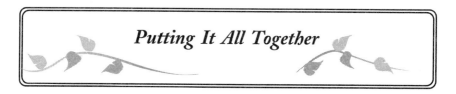

Putting It All Together

In this chapter, three distinct tools have been described. The two card sort tools both lead to values clarification: we use them to create the linkage between money and values and to promote the concept of values in the decision-making process. Using the two card sort tools in tandem allows for a bifocal lens on content and process: the content relates to the values that inform behavior, whereas the process dimension raises awareness about action taken to make and implement decisions. Each card sort exercise is paced and sequenced to lead to a consciousness of values and the linkage to financial decisions. The two card sorts are inherently good tools for awareness and application. The focused genogram tool deepens clients' understanding of the roots of their values and fosters a greater appreciation for transmittal of values as well as motivation toward the transformation process. These three tools enhance facilitation with the client on the continuum of awareness, application, and transformation, offering concreteness and flexibility at the same time. On the one hand, they define words and ideas that allow clients to put ambiguous thought into distinct language. On the other hand, they help the conversation to systematically unfold and allow access to multiple meanings, thus creating the environment for change.

The card sorts and genogram aid professionals in pacing the conversation and sequencing their exploration of money matters to achieve a richer, fuller conversation. The tools can be combined and applied in multiple ways, but the key questions in application are, "How will these tools best serve the client? Which one will move the client from point A to point B?" Coaches or clinicians using the tools need to think about the context for the work, the client's objective, and their relationship to the client or family. The tools provide an expedient entry to what can otherwise be a difficult conversation, while the range of ways to apply them varies from coaching and informal conversation to family meetings and clinical settings.

Chapter 2

Using the Tools to Locate Yourself and Your Self-Awareness

We are all prisoners of our own biographies. The convergence of the professional, familial, and societal realms, each with its own encumbered relationship to money, creates great complexity. The linkage of money and values offers professionals a means to break the silence, facilitate the conversations safely, and access those meanings that can transform their clients' lives. To do this effectively, however, we professionals first must take a multi-dimensional lens and explore the complexities inherent in our own attitudes about money. We have to consider practical, relational, emotional, and attitudinal issues that may include discrepancies between our financial decisions and what we think, say, do, and feel about money. If we can become conscious of our own beliefs and their application to our decisions, then making those decisions can become a way to confront these tensions without the defensive detours we so often take. We need to overcome our fears of entering an arena that has almost always been a taboo subject in many client-professional relationships. Breaking the silence about money with clients requires serious self-reflection by professionals on the meaning of money in their own lives.

Missing the Mark with Clients

Case Study: Tom Misses the Mark

Tom, a colleague, called me to talk about an initial interview for a premarital consult that had not gone well. In fact, the couple never returned, and Tom suspected that he had missed the essence of the problem from a practical and attitudinal perspective. As we spoke, he began to realize that he had skirted the issue of money during the interview, and that money had, in fact, been the primary issue for this couple. Tom came to realize that he needed to explore why he had avoided the money conversation.

Tom recounted the session in the following way: Stacey and Martin had met on an airplane, and their courtship had progressed over the ensuing 18 months. Stacey lived in New York and Martin lived in the Midwest, and they had decided to make a life commitment despite the difference in their religious backgrounds and the discrepancies in their financial resources. They were getting married in a month, after having had numerous conversations about these differences, after speaking to friends and clergy, and after attending various workshops on intermarriage. Everything seemed to be going smoothly. Martin had been able to transfer to the New York office of his firm, and they were living in Stacey's apartment. They had set a wedding date and Stacey's mother was preoccupied with the wedding plans. Two months earlier, however, Stacey's father had handed them a prenuptial agreement at dinner one evening without any warning, completely out of context. They had been stunned by his timing, his awkwardness, and his obvious inability to talk with them about the document. Handing them a sealed manila envelope, he had said briefly, "Please get this signed as soon as possible. The wedding is next month and I need it by then."

Stacey was aghast. She knew her father's policy with any business issue: "Do as I say, no questions asked." Stacey had always resented such infantilization, but this time she was furious. She called her mother in a rage about her father's demand. Her mother, remaining true to her pattern, separated herself from any business issues, abiding by her husband's policy, and trusting that Stacey's father would manage everything. In fact, Stacey's only ally in her desire to become a financially responsible adult was Martin, and this fact created a huge dilemma for her.

They explained all this to Tom in the first twenty minutes of the interview. Instead of focusing on the financial issue and Stacey's conflict with her father, however, Tom chose to explore their religious differences. For Tom, this seemed to be a far more important area for investigation. Stacey and Martin both tried to get the conversation back to the prenuptial agreement and the dilemma of how to proceed. Tom chose to stay with "couple issues" and not get involved with family issues during this first session. As a result, he explored mostly the ways they were thinking about integrating their different religious beliefs into their life together. Tom, thinking they would be able to work on the family relationships at the next session, took the conversation back to the religious issues whenever Stacey and Martin tried to address the issues with Stacey's father. On reflection after the session, Tom began to realize how frustrating this must have been for the couple. In attempting to set a follow-up appointment, he could sense their reluctance and backed off. Tom realized that he had completely missed the issue that was causing them distress. Obviously, the prenuptial agreement was far more disturbing than Tom had assumed. Indeed, from their initial presentation, Tom presumed that they would never have financial worries, and had thought to himself, "How lucky for them!"

Since Tom did not understand the pressures both Stacey and Martin were feeling about having to sign the prenuptial agreement, he never attempted to explore with either of them their reactions to that infamous dinner and the ultimatum from Stacey's father. From Tom's perspective, Martin was a lucky guy, about to marry a lovely woman who happened to have a rich father. What could be bad? The entire conversation that the clients had anticipated initiating in therapy had been derailed because the therapist could not engage in the subject at hand.

Stacey and Martin's story is just one example of a missed conversation. For Tom, the money issue was invisible. But the couple saw their problem with money as real and troubling and wondered, "Why is he not hearing us?" Tom viewed his challenge as turning the conversation from a smoke screen (money) to the underlying emotional issues. Instead of addressing the practical issue, Tom missed his opportunity and tried to engage in what he believed might be a more meaningful entry point to their dilemma. Why did Tom see the money issue as a nonstarter?

The reluctance on the part of this professional to address money issues might be a bias taken from his own family of origin experience, or merely an idea that money is a mundane subject and therefore not worth the time or intellectual thought. As Tom reflected on what had happened with this couple, he began to acknowledge his own resistance to the subject of money. It was this recognition of his own bias that prompted Tom to call me.

Tom's inability to address the money issue with Stacey and Martin highlights the unspoken rule that money is a taboo subject in the clinical space. The reasons for this vary. Some professionals might claim that money is not the real issue, while others might suggest that the underlying meaning is key. The clinician or coach can proffer many rationalizations for this taboo, from philosophical to personal. But the subject is so important a dimension of life that it is time to open the conversation and provide access to the multiple tensions that will inevitably exist for clients on the levels of status, social standing, and security.

Values Clarification Exercise

For many professionals like Tom, the motive to pursue this area might be an experience such as his failed session with Stacey and Martin. As with most issues that have been left unexplored, clinicians and coaches can benefit professionally and personally by widening their lens around financial issues and opening collateral avenues in their professional work. Using the tools described in this book can and will lead to multiple benefits.

When I retrace my personal motivation for exploring issues around money, the most significant benefit for me has been my own shift from powerlessness to empowerment around money and finance. In deconstructing the elements, I realize that knowledge, the language of money and finance, and striving for independence were my three key motivations. When I was a child, my mother taught me about budgeting through my allowance, but my financial education stopped with that. As a young bride, I continued to receive an allowance, but quickly negotiated for a checkbook. My financial independence was one of my main concerns in my divorce. With that in hand, I set out to learn how to ensure my financial security as a single parent responsible for myself and my children. Throughout my life's journey (which has included remarriage and the death of my second husband), knowledge, skills and a values map for guidance have led me toward empowerment, independence, and security. I internalized those values as I continually studied the connections and meanings that money had in my life. My own life experiences have convinced me that explorations for any professional in this arena will almost always prove to be beneficial and enriching.

With the background of Stacey and Martin's story and Tom's recognition of his own issue with money, he and I began our work with a three-part values clarification exercise using the content values card sort. Without mentioning it, I anticipated following up with a money-focused genogram to investigate with him the meaning of money in more depth. Not only would Tom gain greater understanding of his own relationship to money and values, but also he would have these same tools to use in his clinical practice.

I handed Tom the content values card sort, the small deck of 14 cards, each with a value on the top and three bullets underneath that might trigger associations for the value. Tom took the cards and looked at them, commenting that these were all values that seemed to be important to him. I encouraged him to think of the most important three or four values that he would ascribe to himself in contemplating his various roles as husband, father, colleague, and friend. It was critical for Tom to begin with the recognition of his core values—those ideas and attitudes that formed his character. He did the exercise with a sense of curiosity, since he had never been asked these questions before, nor had he thought about using values as a frame of reference for himself or his clients.

Tom identified four values as his core values: "relationships," "spirituality," "ethical values," and "education". Asking him a few questions to focus on these issues, I gave him the space to address the personal side. Did these values reflect who he was and how he spent his time? Was there congruency or dissonance between the ways he thought about himself and his actions in terms of his time and money? Were these values he practiced, or were they values reflecting how he would like to think of himself—an idealized, rather than a realized version of self?

Pondering my questions for a while, Tom slowly made the distinctions. First, he claimed that there was congruence between how he thought about himself and how he acted. He then proudly noted that there was little gap between his idealized self and his true self, citing concrete examples of how his actions matched these values.

Shifting to the interpersonal dimension of the exercise, I asked him to consider whether his wife and grown children, in doing the sort on his behalf, would describe him with the same four values. Tom thought that everyone in his family would describe him as he pictured himself. I then noted that he had not selected any cards related specifically to money such as financial responsibility or economics. He responded quickly and said, "Of course. That's because I do not see money as important."

What I have observed with my professional colleagues is that they tend not to focus on the financial dimensions of life. This is in stark contrast to my own experience, in which the subject has been front and center throughout my family life. It does not surprise me that my professional focus has gravitated to this area, given my own life experiences; what does surprise me is the glaring gap in focus by my colleagues.

I have tried to consider rationales for this noninterest in the subject of money. The professional's attitude seems to promote the "helping agenda" over and above "material things" and "social status"— the emotional makeup of clients (the focus of most therapy) is seen as separate from their financial situation. Money might be considered important only for managing one's life, but taboo in any other context. Whatever the attitude, exploring the underpinnings is important.

Access to family of origin data and process will certainly reveal the genesis and evolution of the attitudes.

To move Tom in that direction, I decided to shift to the application exercise, which focuses on applying values to financial decisions. I asked him to think back to the most recent big financial decision he had made (e.g., refinancing a mortgage, moving, changing a job, or purchasing a second home). After a few minutes, Tom looked up and nodded his head suggesting he had a decision in mind. I then asked him to reshuffle the cards and sort them so that we could talk about the values he used to inform his decision making. Tom chose three cards that were somewhat different from his core values: economics, education, and relationships. Tom described the educational fund he had just set up for his grandchildren on the advice of his accountant. He had recently been blessed with the birth of his first grandchild but thought that his spontaneous response to his accountant's suggestion had been based on pure economics. We looked at his first card sort results and realized that there was some overlap between the two sets. Tom commented that education, which had always been a core value for him, was one of those values that informed his financial decision to set up the fund. As we continued to discuss the decision, Tom expressed surprise at how his values had informed his decision. Although his accountant had suggested setting up the fund as a prudent tax-planning move, Tom had certainly integrated other values for himself into the decision.

In applying the values exercise to a real-life decision, the consciousness of the connection between thought and action surfaced. For some reason, Tom had always dealt with money as a separate issue, and one, moreover, that he preferred not to think about. And because of this resistance, he had never before connected them to his values although he had made multiple financial decisions throughout his adult life. The discrepancy for Tom related to his inability to make the connection between money and values. This is often an "aha" moment for participants in the exercise—when the meaning of money with a negative connotation shifts to more positive ones. When people give themselves permission to think about money with expanded positive assumptions and this shift has a real impact on the personal and the interpersonal dimensions, it can be a poignant revelation. Making the connection between financial decision making and values opens the channel of communication in the relational context. It gives structure, safety, and pride to the conversation. It gives a new frame of reference for the money conversation, which otherwise is too often polluted by emotional connections.

This card sort allows clients to access their emotional reactions to money. By using values as a frame of reference, the participants become aware of their emotional connections to the money agenda. For many, the context created with the card sort feels safe, which allows for more extensive discussion and deliberation. This naturally leads to improved communication.

Tom was pleased to recognize that the values in the first exercise did in fact correlate with those in the second. Again, much to his surprise, he enjoyed the reflective conversation that ensued. Talking about money in this way expanded the discussion, presenting a much wider range for consideration and dissipating the negative connotations that, for him, frequently accompanied discussions about money.

Next, I handed Tom a new set of cards and introduced him to the process values concept. In doing so, I reviewed the cards with him and explained that these were not necessarily the same for all clients, explaining that the *how* of our decision making is as significant as the *why*. Our goal in developing these cards as a tool is to have people become conscious of their decision making and implementation processes around the financial dimension of their lives, thus addressing the interpersonal aspects and the accompanying dissonance or congruence.

Tom looked at the nine cards and immediately turned ashen. He was unable to hide his reaction and noted quickly that although he liked to think of himself as collaborative and engaged others in decision making in most dimensions of his life, he never discussed his financial decisions with anybody. He never spoke to anyone, never asked opinions other than from his accountant, and never explained his thinking to anyone in his family. When it came to finances, Tom handled decisions in a traditional, hierarchical manner. With chagrin, Tom thought back to Stacey's father handing her the prenuptial agreement. He quickly recognized why he had not responded to Stacey's story. Her father's behavior had congruency with his own, even though he would have denied the hierarchical card as his stance. As this surfaced for Tom, he sat still in his seat, stunned at this new self-revelation.

This naturally led him to consider two issues relating to money. The first was his reluctance to talk about it in the clinical space. The second was his personal style of financial decision making. Tom wanted to explore why he could manage his own financial life with a set of values that informed his own decisions, yet resist using this as an entry point for a money discussion in his clinical practice. He noted a clear visceral reaction to the suggestion that he pursue this topic with clients. He was still not convinced that money talk was an important issue to raise clinically even though, in his practice, he frequently encountered couples arguing about it and individuals obsessing over it.

This encounter may raise more questions than answers. Many people in the helping professions place caring for others over and above any financial agenda. Thus, for many of us, money is not a part of the clinical conversation, even though we deal with the issue in our own lives, paying our bills, managing our practices, planning for retirement, building our nest eggs. In essence, we value economic responsibility in our own lives, but somehow do not want to think of financial responsibility as a core value. This results in excluding the money agenda from our conversations with clients.

The eye-opener for the professional is the application of the concept of process. As therapists, we are trained to watch the process and apply it in our clinical assessment. We rarely focus on what our own idealized process values are and whether we actually use them. The concept of process values is fairly new, and the discrepancy that manifests in this way may make it harder to surface. It introduces people to the concept along with their personal accountability.

Two things became apparent to Tom. First, he did think about the money issue in his own life, but switched that dimension of himself off in his clinical space. Second, the process he used personally was hierarchical, a position he had never realized or examined. He readily agreed to my suggestion to explore his family history to see if we could understand the premises that informed his reaction to the money topic, and was amenable to our doing a money-focused genogram to trace how his family dealt with money. This would give us access to the attitudes and emotional connections that Tom had probably encountered and internalized, and would help us understand Tom's visceral reaction.

Tom's Genogram

Working on Tom's genogram using the questions mentioned in Chapter 1, what surfaced was his parents' consistent conflict over money. His father struggled to earn a decent living, but his mother was never satisfied. She had come from an upper-middle-class home, and his father had pulled himself up from life in a tenement. As a child, Tom picked up the message of disappointment and frustration conveyed by his mother to and about his father. No matter what Tom's father did, or how much he earned, it was not good enough for his mother because she had imagined that she would live a life of comfort, without worries about financial issues. Her great disappointment was that Tom's father had never succeeded in "climbing up the career ladder" so that they would not have to constantly worry about money. His mother was always critical and disrespectful of his father, and Tom had hated how she had talked to him, especially when they argued about money.

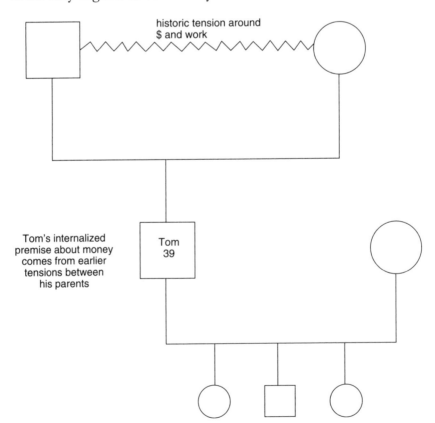

As a child, Tom had identified with his dad during these arguments and was sensitive to the shame his father had felt. In experiencing this sensitivity as a child, Tom had not known what to do about it, but he had made a conscious decision early in his life never to talk about money with anyone, since such conversations would only trigger criticism and disrespect. From early childhood, Tom had chosen to avoid any money conversation as his solution to the emotional tension within his family. He had held that position from boyhood to the present, noting that he handled the finances in his family and never discussed money with his wife, who trusted him implicitly in this area. All he had ever done was tell her how much money she could spend. She never questioned him, as she had never wanted to pay attention to finances and was content to live with the knowledge that she and Tom had a comfortable life together.

When such a strong emotional attachment to an idea is held so firmly, it is difficult to influence change. When there is anxiety and stress in the family system, children may try to absorb or manage that stress by developing solutions to the problem. These solutions become premises that may stay with a person especially when they have been effective in neutralizing the original anxiety state. Changing these premises requires patience and fortitude, since we all are ambivalent about change. The forces within us to change or stay the same are constant, and the fear of what will fill the gap is profound.

Tom quickly understood where this process was taking him. As a clinician, he knew that the premise he had developed as a child had been his solution to dealing with his parents' marital tension. He commented that he actually did not take anyone's side in this argument, having come to a solution that he thought was "above the fray." He liked recognizing that in himself. At the same time, he recognized how this premise had led to his avoiding money issues in both his personal and professional life. Having established his hierarchical way of dealing with his family finances, we explored together how he had created an emotional wall when it came to money talk. This happened in his marriage, with his children, and with colleagues as well as his clients. Tom saw that his resistance to the money talk had pervaded all his relationships. Looking at me with a smile on his face at the end of our session, Tom thanked me for helping him unlock this door. He understood that it would have wide implications for him as he struggled with the conscious effort to change himself.

Tom's challenge was to change his emotional response to money along with its underlying meaning to him. For others, the challenge might be related to shifting the meaning of a value or attitude attached to money and the required transformation of that value to a different context.

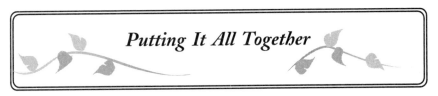

Putting It All Together

The tools presented in this chapter encourage a sequential process, first creating awareness of values, then facilitating application, and finally promoting transformation. The principal objective for therapists or coaches is to find their own meaning of money so that conversations with clients become more natural. When using this methodology, the clinician has to facilitate the pacing of the exercises and move the focus from the values dimension to the emotional process within which that occurs. Guiding clients within those fields becomes the art that leads to the desired transformation and change.

Although Tom's primary motive as a child was to rid himself of the uncomfortable feeling of shame to which he was so sensitive, for others, the underlying affect might be fear or powerlessness. The goal need not always be to access these motives, since for many people acquiring the values, language alone is enough to begin breaking the silence. For coaches, this achievement might break through a barrier and begin to shift a premise. For clinicians, these tools provide a road map to the conversation in a defined format. They access a subject that may have untapped meaning. They present a format for values promotion as a lifetime frame and can guide the process toward transformational change.

For the clinician who has used these tools, the shift that takes place is often from a position of silence on the subject of money to a more open and accessible conversation about finances in the clinical space. For the coach, it has similar impact in opening the conversation with clients. When working with professionals, the outcome has led to an expanded understanding of how to think about money, a greater comfort talking about money and, as a result, the ease for application in their practices.

If Tom could replay his initial interview with Stacey and Martin, we can assume that he would respond differently to their story, especially concerning the incident with Stacey's father. Instead of ignoring the story and moving into another area, Tom would probably engage with them about the prenuptial agreement despite its complexity in both content and process. He would then move the conversation from the prenuptial agreement toward the new concept of a values-based approach to their financial partnership as a dimension of their upcoming marriage. From this segue, Tom might introduce the values card sort, which would have led to a conversation that, in turn, might have become the foundation for a productive conversation with Stacey's father and future conversations throughout their marriage.

As a result of his new consciousness about the relationship between money and values, Tom felt more comfortable engaging in the dialogue and exploring the issues related to the financial dimension of life using a values perspective. Tom learned how he could shift the focus of the conversation about money alone to a more meaningful one about values and money, a connection that he now perceived as relevant.

Soon after Tom and I completed our sessions together, he called me to report another experience in his clinical practice. He had received a call from Kim, a woman he had counseled a while back who had been through a divorce. She was now dating someone seriously and she was looking toward remarriage. Her concern was the financial discrepancy between her and her partner, and she wanted to talk about this with Tom. She was having trouble addressing this dimension of their future life together. Eager to try out his new tools, Tom agreed to see them for a consultation.

Tom welcomed Kim and Paul into his office. He had spoken to Kim and now wanted to hear Paul's perception of why they had decided to see him. Paul told Tom that he was divorced with a child from his first marriage and a financial obligation to his son and ex-wife.

He and Kim had decided to get married, but neither one felt comfortable pursuing the conversation about their future financial arrangements. Paul stated that he had never been very good at such conversation in his first marriage and did not want to repeat the same quarrels with Kim over money that he had experienced with his ex-wife. Kim was not comfortable talking about these issues either, so to open the conversation, they had both decided to try talking with Tom about their future financial partnership.

Tom told them about the new methodology he had learned and suggested they try it. He introduced the concept of a values-based approach to financial decision making and started by handing them the card sort and asking each of them to define their individual values. The good news was that they shared many of the same values. This naturally reinforced their positive feelings about their future together. The next step was the application of values to their most recent financial decision. Kim and Paul did this exercise separately as they were still living apart and had separate financial obligations. Tom then introduced the concept of the process values.

Throughout the exercises, Tom was amazed at how comfortable he felt with asking questions and probing each client in the areas that would lead to further understanding. Both Kim and Paul were surprised at what they were learning about each other. Paul articulated his concerns about Kim's expectations that their roles in this marriage would continue to be the traditional ones each had experienced the first time around. Paul wanted a partner with whom he could set up a financial plan annually, who would be knowledgeable in budgeting, and who would understand how much they could and could not spend. He also wanted a partner who would not shy away from the conversation. He wanted to be able to make decisions that reflected how they both wanted to shape and live their life. He understood that they would not always agree and that certain disparities in their expectations might exist since Kim had grown accustomed to some of the finer things in life. He also knew that he could not always afford to give her these things and wanted complete transparency.

Kim had been managing her own finances for the past five years since her divorce and did not want to give that up because she had become much more comfortable with making choices about purchases, vacations, and other expenses. Her real concern was that Paul would want to take over and prevent her from continuing the management role she had come to enjoy. Both her father and her first husband had maintained the power and control over decisions with money, and she had never had financial autonomy until she was divorced. She wanted to retain this autonomy, but also had a preconceived idea of the man as the financial decision maker, and was confused by this disparity.

Paul and Kim's inability to have an open conversation about these issues had been based on the unwarranted assumptions that each had about the other. The ability to communicate about these conflicting premises in a constructive, safe environment that Tom had created with the values cards was a positive experience for them individually and as a couple. The recognition that they shared essential values helped them acknowledge the solidity of the multiple dimensions of their future partnership in friendship, romance, and business.

Tom called me to discuss the session. He was amazed at how meaningful the conversation had been for this couple. He was also surprised by his own comfort level in facilitating the conversation between them, remembering how he had abbreviated these conversations in the past by avoiding the money issue and moving onto something else. The session had neutralized the escalating tension that neither Kim nor Paul knew how to address and that could have negatively affected their future together. He also noted that they were ecstatic to have a road map for their present and future financial planning, based on values rather than on frustration and disappointment. Tom's experience of this interview was completely different from the one he had with Stacey and Martin. Now that he had tools to use when it came to money talk, he no longer needed to shy away from the subject. He understood that if he met his clients at the juncture of money and family life, he could move from the problem area to awareness and change more effectively.

The tension between power and powerlessness is prominent in most scenarios where money is a factor. Application of this methodology to our personal and professional lives provides a way to grapple with the multiple issues that surface for each of us around the meaning of money. The interface between our personal and professional experiences is consistently at play. The clearer we can be about the issues for ourselves, the better we can help our clients.

PART 2

Conversations about Money in the Relational Context

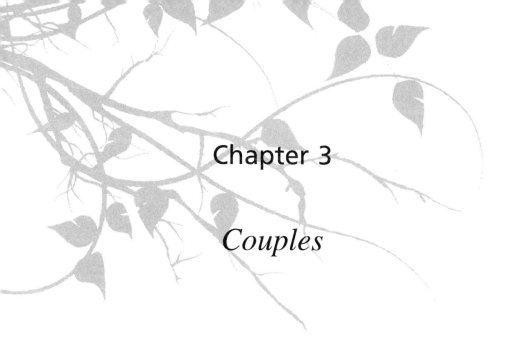

Chapter 3

Couples

The combination of money and marriage can create many powerful associations. Money impacts the power balance in marital relationships individually and interpersonally, profoundly affecting the couple's life together. As seen with the couples who consulted Tom, a therapist or coach who is not sensitized and ready to discuss these multiple meanings will miss opportunities for assessment and exploration of the complexities inherent in the marital relationship.

To highlight the application of these tools in dealing with money and marriage, the case studies in this chapter present three couples, each at a different stage of life. We employ our tools with a specific focus for each couple to demonstrate how a values-based approach to money talk can access and help resolve marital conflicts. In using the card sort process, our three objectives are awareness, implementation, and transformation. All three phases of the card sort process can be facilitated sequentially in one meeting or separately in a series of meetings.

David and Olivia, the first couple, are in the early stages of marriage. Their story involves the awareness of their individual and shared values. The application of these values for their financial decision making becomes a constructive process as they begin their life's journey together, providing a road map for their financial discussions and helping them to avoid arguments around money in the future. Art and Yvonne, the second couple, are looking toward their retirement. They are stuck in transition and the accompanying change of pattern in their decision making. With this couple, the focus is on their implementation and the acknowledgment that a shift in their relational dynamic has caused multiple emotional reactions. Using the card sort gives them structure, language, and access to the difficulties that accompany the change process. They gain greater clarity of their issues and move toward resolution. Jim and Claire, the third couple, are older and are struggling to adapt a value held closely for their lifetime to a new set of circumstances. Faced with the challenge of transformation, they are assessing the impact on their relationship.

Awareness

Case Study: David and Olivia Plan Their Financial Philosophy

David and Olivia have been married for a year. Before their wedding, they had talked about the multifaceted nature of marriage. They thought they had covered every dimension of their future friendship, romance, and business partnership. Now, they found themselves constantly arguing about money. Every weekend ended with a quarrel around spending too much money. David wanted to save for a home, while Olivia wanted to spend money to make their present home comfortable for entertaining. David never wanted to invite people over because he was concerned about their budget, whereas Olivia wanted to have fun with family and friends. They found themselves in a constant tug of war. Olivia mentioned this problem to a friend who recommended they see a professional who specialized in working with families and couples on money issues.

Despite all the conversation around their future that occurs when two people decide to build a life together and get married, what is often absent from those discussions is a financial philosophy and plan. Creating a joint financial philosophy can be a simple process that the couple revisits and reworks as life's journey brings with it different challenges and priorities. For the couple, this requires reflective thought and conversation. Using values as the basis for developing this plan provides a solid foundation and helps couples in making the decisions that will ultimately shape their lives.

David and Olivia entered my office, sat down, and described their problems. I asked if they had ever talked about a financial philosophy for shaping their life together and when they responded with a resounding "No!" I proposed that we attempt to do that together. They balked at my suggestion, but when I explained that we would begin by having them define their individual and shared values, they agreed. I went on to explain that this would help them articulate what was important to them, the first step in creating a financial philosophy together. Once they understood the purpose behind my suggestion, they agreed to the exercise.

I handed David and Olivia the content values card sort. They looked at one another, clearly intrigued with the exercise. Following my instructions to sort the deck into those values that were most important and those that were least important, they confronted the task of finding the core values—those ideas and beliefs that informed their behavior throughout their many identities. I directed them to do the exercise individually, without discussion or comments.

Most couples respond positively to this exercise. The challenge is to focus on the self and articulate their own self definitions. Beyond the more common practice of self definition through perceived identities and personality traits, defining the self by articulating one's value system adds the dimension of character to the exploration of self and provides a moral compass. The most difficult part of the exercise is not talking to one's partner about it while sorting the cards, since the individual perspective is critical to the ongoing process.

Most professionals strive to create a safe context for conversation in the clinical space and the content values card sort helps accomplish this goal. While specifying definitions for self identity is daunting for some clients, the concept and language of values is calming because of its positive connotation. Clients can discuss issues and realities in a nonconfrontational way. Although couples occasionally end this exercise angry and upset, in my experience that has rarely been the case. Almost always, after identifying and sharing their values, the couple walks away reconfirming the bonds that attracted them initially.

It took David and Olivia several minutes to acclimate and prioritize. Olivia was more interested in the exercise than David, noting that although the task was difficult, she was determined to choose her top four. At one point, she asked if she could choose five, and when told she could not, finally finished, eager to share her choices. David remained skeptical about the value of this exercise. Olivia described her values, in no special order, as "relationships," "spirituality," "ethical values," and "physical needs." She explained that her daily actions as a teacher, daughter, wife, sister, and friend reflected these values. Throughout her life, she maintained that these issues had been "front burner" for her and still gave her life meaning.

David seemed surprised to hear Olivia articulate these ideas so clearly. He understood that these characteristics had made her so attractive to him, but acknowledged that he had never actually focused on them in this way. He had chosen "ethical values," "physical needs," "financial responsibility," and "work" as his top four values. He quickly perceived that the similarities and differences in their choices explained why there were tensions between them. For one thing, he simply did not value relationships as she did, and commented that he depended on her to manage that dimension of their lives. As he talked about it, he recognized that this was how his parents handled their relationship. Similarly, Olivia noted that she had copied her parents' patterns around finance and work. Although they claimed not to have a traditional marriage, they understood from this conversation how each had assumed traditional gendered roles. They smiled at each other as this reality set in.

The next step in the card sort exercise was for David and Olivia to apply their values-based approach to their financial decision making. I encouraged them to consider their most recent big financial decision. Because they had only been married for a year, they had not yet made any major financial decisions together and were still trying to work out an annual budget. After identifying their basic expenses of food, shelter, and clothing, they repeatedly got stuck trying to allocate their remaining funds, and this impasse had, in fact, been the catalyst that brought them into the office. The exercise shifted, then, from a financial decision to a budgeting question. Each had brought a copy of a budget they had made independently—their first attempt to solve their problem. Using their separate budgets as a frame of reference, David and Olivia did the card sort and identified the top values that had informed their proposals.

The conversation that ensued was not surprising. David's top priorities were "economics," "material possessions," and "relationships." He noted how completely different these values were from those he had chosen in the first exercise, and was surprised both by the discrepancy and by his choice of the relational value card this time. He explained that saving for the home he desperately wanted was rooted in his strong vision of their future family life. Although he had not described himself in the first exercise as having relationships as a core value, he realized, after doing this exercise, how much that value informed his desire and commitment to save for their future home. Olivia questioned his commitment to this value in application but the absence of it in his core value choice, and this stymied David as well.

Olivia was visibly touched by this conversation. For a poignant moment, they looked at each other and then hugged. Then Olivia showed David her cards. She had chosen some values similar to his, and David was shocked that she had also used economic value to inform her decision. David had begun to believe that Olivia was spoiled and acted like a child, especially about financial matters. They talked about their bickering but with a completely different attitude, beginning to appreciate how they had gotten offtrack in these fights. They were both completely committed to their shared goal of having a family and saving for a home. Their conflict had been around the short term and the "how to" agenda of their mutual goal. They realized then that they could create compromises and still work toward their shared goal.

The shift from tension and conflict to recognition of shared values usually brings about awareness for the couple of the common ground on which they entered their union. Couples who marry have a multitude of connections—some that are obvious and overt and others that remain covert. The couple may share an unidentified value system, and this connection can potentially be significant as they travel life's paths together. The card sort helps them identify this value system and give it precedence. This awareness in turn provides a road map for the present and future, becoming a tool they can access as the need arises.

If a couple discovers that they have no connection or overlap of their basic values, they are confronted with the awareness of this dissonance and disjunction. The challenge becomes negotiating these differences. Along with the consciousness of their discrepancies comes the opportunity to manage the process and be more constructive in their conversations.

Defining individual and shared values provides a language and structure for communication and clarity in ongoing conversations. It also establishes a platform for a process leading to compromise, and the ability to "agree to disagree," while neutralizing tensions connected to financial decisions. Finally, defining their values helps clients achieve a broader understanding of money and a blueprint for future financial decision making. This new, shared language can neutralize the tensions that arise during the early years of marriage, when couples embark on the journey of shaping their future together.

Implementation

Once a couple identifies their values and are able to use them as a blueprint for their ongoing decision making, the next challenge they face is to actually implement their plan. Putting their values and priorities into practice can lead to misunderstandings. When working with couples, it is important for the therapist or coach to recognize this area of possible discrepancy. As in most planning and practice, the implementation is an art rather than a science, and the coach must let the principles and values serve as the guideposts.

Case Study: Art and Yvonne Plan for Retirement

Art and Yvonne have been together for over 20 years. She had worked in an accounting firm as the office manager and was looking forward to retirement. He had been driving a taxi for the same amount of time and had accumulated a nest egg for their retirement years. They both knew that they wanted to stop working within the next five years, but had never thought about how they wanted to live or what they wanted to do in retirement. They had discussed options, but somehow had repeatedly gotten stuck when contemplating putting their plan into action. Coming into the office, they began to speak about the dilemma they faced in figuring out what to do with the next phase of their lives. They agreed that they were getting ready to retire, but could not get past that initial decision. Whenever they started to talk about their future plans, the conversation escalated into an argument. The disagreement was not about retiring, but there was, nonetheless, something about the topic that consistently set off an explosion.

Although many couples agree on the content values they share, often there are overlaps rather than exact alignment. A discussion about content values is always an important initial conversation as a point of reference for future conversations that connect money and values. The conflict for couples often surfaces in the area of implementation. Couples get into a pattern of financial decisions without any consciousness of their own process. They might start out with a shared value, the way Art and Yvonne both looked forward to retirement, and as partners, they automatically follow the pattern they have used previously for implementation. The difficulty surfaces when one partner wants to change the pattern without acknowledging and communicating that desire. The conversation gets detoured and all sorts of issues get raised that have little to do with the objective at hand.

Art and Yvonne had always made their financial decisions together, but Art was the one who followed up and implemented their decisions. This had become a problem for Yvonne. At the age of 60, she was becoming concerned that she was not fully informed about their financial life. Art did not understand why she asked so many questions. Did she not trust him anymore? She had always left those responsibilities to him and now, suddenly, she was asking him about every detail of every financial transaction. He was, frankly, sick and tired of her questions, and they fought constantly about this. He complained that their life had turned into a nightmare. She nagged, and he reacted by blowing up. Then, silence prevailed. How were they going to continue like this? Their future retirement had changed from a dream to a torturous struggle. They were at the end of their marital rope.

Couples are not always sensitized to the dynamic of their relationship. The interaction between them—the unspoken and undefined rules and roles—sets a pattern with individual and interpersonal ramifications. The pattern becomes the blueprint for the relationship, and the desire on the part of one partner to change it can become a catalyst for disruption and conflict.

Art and Yvonne had been dealing with their financial decisions together for 20 years. They were unaware of the gender-based roles they had assumed. They would talk about their life together, setting out their priorities, and then Art would manage the implementation. It had worked for Yvonne for all these years, since she took care of the household and managed their recreational life as well as holding down a full-time job. When she introduced questions, however, Art began to worry about her motivation and why she was challenging his position as the man in the family. And although he had never articulated his concern, Art was apprehensive about the status of their marriage and whether Yvonne might be thinking about leaving him. He could never broach the subject, but he viewed the questions she asked about their financial situation as proof of his suspicions.

When a pattern changes in a relationship without any obvious reason, the change can cause intense anxiety. Whether the cause is defined or has a more amorphous quality, it can be difficult for the parties to identify its source. The challenge for the couple, as well as the therapist, is to recognize that a change has taken place and to identify where, when, and why it happened. Using the values construct exercise can help exploration.

In listening to Yvonne and Art's narrative, I was struck that the situation had changed so abruptly just three or four months ago. I decided not to pursue the timing of the change at that moment, resolving to return to it later. Instead, I asked them to look at the values cards and do the card sort. They did this quickly, and as I would have anticipated, they were aware of the similarities and differences in their individual choices. The second step in the card sort, the application to financial decision making, went smoothly as well. They both chose their decision to retire as their issue, and applied similar values to that decision.

I then moved to the process values card sort to try to uncover the source of Art and Yvonne's conflict. Yvonne chose "transparency," "collaboration," and "dialogue" as her values and saw that she was looking for an open process with Art around their planning and implementation. Art, on the other hand, had chosen "hierarchy," "exclusivity," and "dialogue"—cards that actually highlighted their differences. Art explained that the dialogue card he had chosen referred to his informing Yvonne of what he was doing and how they were progressing toward their goal. The other two cards represented how they had been handling these matters for the past 20 years. As Art articulated it, they would come to a global decision, and he would take charge, figuring out the best way for them to achieve their goal. He was in charge of implementation and only asked questions if he got stuck. Yvonne counted on his expertise and thoroughness, and he felt that he was fulfilling his role as the man of the house.

In identifying these process values, the couple recognized what their struggle was really about. Only then could they have a conversation about their differences, the underlying premises that informed those differences, and the emotional reactions they had each experienced by the shift that was taking place in their relationship. Thus, the final card sort helped them gain access to their interpersonal dynamic with a new, revealing lens.

The motivation for Yvonne's shift surfaced during the conversation around the card sort, and as that happened, Art's anxiety decreased. Yvonne finally explained her feelings in a way that she had never before articulated to Art. Her anxiety was connected to the possible need for her to manage her life independently one day. Since their unspoken contract about how they handled money seemed to have multiple meanings for Art, Yvonne had never been able to raise the subject without creating controversy.

Art and Yvonne recognized that the gender role he assumed early in their marriage, which included the responsibility of implementing all their family financial decisions, caused him to feel like the head of the house and thus connected his manliness to this activity. After their constructive conversation, he understood why Yvonne had asked so many questions. She was not challenging his management, but rather attempting to alleviate her own anxiety. Although Art did not want to give up his role in their financial life, he now understood why Yvonne had persisted in asking questions and recognized that he had to transform his perception of his responsibilities.

We then arrived at the issue that I had shelved early on in our meeting: What had caused this need for change several months earlier? I learned that around that time, Yvonne's good friend Jan had lost her husband after a protracted illness. Yvonne had watched Jan struggle to get her financial life in order. Because Jan had been uninformed about her financial life throughout her marriage, she faced a steep learning curve after her husband's death. Yvonne noted her friend's distress and decided, without discussing it with Art, that she would educate herself about their financial matters now, while she and Art were both alive and healthy. Instead of sharing her concerns about her lack of knowledge of their financial situation with Art, she merely began, on a sporadic basis, to ask questions. Their unspoken rule had been that Art was in charge, and there were no money discussions. By asking questions, Yvonne was attempting to maintain their rules and roles while alleviating her anxiety. Art had interpreted her questions as challenging his competency and manhood, and this led to an emotional reaction for both of them. It became easier to fight than to confront the sensitive issues of potential loss, competence, and power. Using these exercises enabled them to have an informative, productive conversation about money and their future financial plan. The card sort allowed them to differentiate between actual money issues and their relational context.

These tools created a safe environment where the couple could focus on the shift in the pattern of their relationship. In addition, the tools hastened the process for engaging in the conversation, helping them to recognize the underlying individual issues and their impact on their interactions. The points of dissonance became apparent quickly, and it was no longer taboo to talk about financial planning. All of this was Step 1 for Art and Yvonne. Step 2 would involve the exploration of options for change.

Art and Yvonne's common goal of retirement and recreation established the basis for the conversation. For them, the dynamic shift was not situated in the life goal, but in their long-term dynamic pattern. Yvonne's desire to be financially informed for her personal sense of security was a new issue, and Art would need to shift both his understanding about her need for this knowledge as well as his own role in the process, from a hierarchical to an empowering stance. In continued conversations, they began to understand how their gendered roles had affected them, and just as importantly, they discovered a safe way to talk about this topic. The fighting stopped, the anxiety was neutralized, and they could expedite their life plan.

When the taboo of money talk is eliminated and the emotions connected to money surface, the challenge for the therapist or coach becomes how to identify the desired change. For an individual or couple, shifting a long-time premise requires a conscious choice, and the card sort serves as a method for uncovering the rationale behind that choice. For many therapists, the card sort leads back to their home ground of facilitation and exploration of issues and their significance. This will likely cause the conflicts to surface as well as the ideas that can suggest a desired transformation. The card sort can expedite this conversation and provide a construct for further discussion about power, guilt, and shame, the all-too-often emotional connections to money.

For Art and Yvonne, the value that opened up the conversation was "empowerment." Yvonne had chosen "transparency," "collaboration," and "dialogue" as her top three choices. But in investigating what had shifted for her, she looked at the cards again and realized that she was trying to learn more about these money matters for her sense of safety. For years, Art had handled their financial matters, and she wanted him to teach her what he did so that she would not feel vulnerable should anything happen to him. They understood that their initial pattern with financial matters had been hierarchical as well as patriarchal, and both of them needed to acknowledge that a change had to take place in the premise attached to that pattern. The values card had given Yvonne the language to articulate her motivation in a way that did not threaten their relational connection.

Transformation

Therapists and coaches serve as change agents in a collaborative process with their clients. The objective of therapy is to help clients take an idea that they have held and revisit that idea given a new context. The challenge then becomes how to create the transformation of the premise based on the new reality.

In doing this work, the constant effort is learning how to align thoughts, actions, and feelings. Questioning the premises that have informed their behavior guides clients to explore the relevance of lifelong values for their current situation. This exploration can lead to transformation—a difficult process because it requires consistent recognition of where the disjunction occurs. Because the inherent pattern is familiar and comfortable, the greatest complexity develops when individuals must change their understanding of an idea that has informed their lives for a long time while remaining aware of interpersonal dynamics. Even for those who are conscious of the issues, it is more than likely that the old patterns will resurface, especially around areas that have been frozen or unexplored, as is often the case with money matters. Having a couple explore these issues together illuminates their joint desire to change the patterns of their relationship, and thus help each other through that change.

Therapists and coaches can use the card sort as a tool to address the transformational process with their clients. By engaging in conversation about these values, I have been constantly reminded of how initial ideas become embedded in people's minds. Resistance to changing that initial understanding of a particular value informs one's behavior even though life circumstances have changed and the value, as one has lived it, might require reassessment.

Case Study: Jim and Claire Change Their Pattern

Jim and Claire had been married for 45 years, and their marriage was a successful one, with each person enjoying personal space and time. They both grew up in middle-class homes, and their lives together had been informed by a strong work ethic as well as by the economic value of frugality. Jim had developed a successful business and sold it at a substantial profit. They retired with the proceeds, and both became involved in church activities, conducting their new volunteer life much as they had conducted their working lives. Their new daily routine allowed them to transform their work ethic value as well as adapt their economic value of frugality. They had transitioned their "long-term partnership" from the world of work to the world of retirement and volunteerism.

Many couples live their lives together in patterns that provide a comfort zone for the degree of intimacy that is right for them. This is represented in the delicate balance that couples navigate between separateness and connectedness. The context within which this pattern exists can change with life circumstances, but if such couples can maintain the dynamic, life can continue as it has in the past.

All was working well for Jim and Claire until one day Jim, who was in his early eighties, fell. His injuries, although not incapacitating, had a detrimental effect on their relationship. Jim could no longer lead his independent life and looked to Claire to be with him every moment. Claire experienced his desire to have her by his side as suffocating. She felt tension between her guilt and sense of responsibility to Jim on the one hand and her anxiety from too much togetherness on the other hand, and she did not know how to handle this tension.

When something occurs that disrupts a couple's pattern, the challenge becomes adaptation. Some couples are resilient, and can shift their dynamic without much dissonance. Others have great difficulty in making the adjustment in the relational balance.

Jim and Claire could not adapt to the consequences of Jim's accident. The discord in their relationship evolved over months as the pattern of their life shifted. They stopped going to their daily church activities. They spent much of their time going to doctors' appointments together. Claire was in charge of Jim's care. Although she had household support, she nonetheless experienced the change as confining. She could not figure out how to balance her old life with the new reality of Jim's physical limitations. They were confined to their home, which led to constant bickering. Jim wanted them to be together continually, and Claire struggled with her own mixed and confused reactions.

To anyone who would listen, Claire stated repeatedly that she felt as though she had lost her life, describing herself as someone who had become caught in a maze. Whereas she and Jim had adapted smoothly to retirement with some first-order change, they were having difficulties adjusting to this latest event. The shift in their external circumstances made it impossible to maintain the dynamic pattern they had enjoyed for so many years.

Knowing Claire and Jim for many years as a consultant/advisor for their philanthropic initiatives, I asked Claire to consider whether she had lost her personal time or her whole life. She looked at me intently, her attention caught by the distinction I had made. With this distinction, I thought that perhaps the problem might seem more tangible and could be addressed with a structured approach.

I suggested that she carve out more personal time for herself, and we began to explore ways she could do that. Jim, listening to the conversation, assured her that he did not mind if she left him during the day, but wanted to go with her when she went out in the evenings. Claire reminded him how difficult it was for them to get around. During this conversation, which had to do with structure and boundaries for them as a couple, I suggested that they hire someone to drive them in the evenings. Both of them responded in chorus that this was not how they lived their lives, that they would not spend money in that way. I was struck by their response and realized that the frozen shared value of frugality was impeding their ability to cope with their new reality and realign their relational harmony.

Frequently in working with couples, the therapist encounters multiple tensions in the couple's process or in their underlying values. When the focus of a conversation is an option that might bring about transformation and lead to a different experience for the couple, their resistance is unusually bound up in the frozen shared assumption. Thus, the first step with Claire and Jim was to acknowledge that their shared economic value of frugality had been a foundational asset and solid base for their life together. Next, it was important to help them reevaluate how this idea might inform their lives today, posing the idea that their situation had changed and therefore might require a different perspective on frugality. As a couple well into the next chapter of their life together, Jim and Claire had done very well for themselves on the economic front.

They had planned for giving back to their community, and they had taken care of their family. At this juncture, they had to consider the quality of their own lives. According to the information they had given me, they did not have to worry about their finances, and the economic value that had guided them for so long might require some tweaking. I also pointed out, in concrete terms, the financial implications of my suggestion. They were a bit startled by my analysis, but got the point immediately. The next time I saw them, they told me that they had taken my suggestion and, as a result, had had some lovely cultural evenings out together.

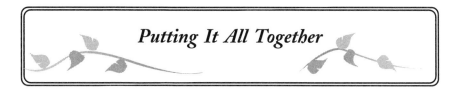

Putting It All Together

Coaches or consultants, as opposed to therapists, have more pronounced opportunities to influence a change process. Consultants have the freedom to voice the contradiction between a client's stated principle or value and the person's actions within the context and can use it as a catalyst to change. Because consultants are focused on rational (nonemotional) issues, they can facilitate the conversation with fewer tensions. This does not always result in the change process, but it does open up the door to reflective thinking.

Transformation takes place when a person begins to think about an old idea in a new way. Too many people become rigid about the ideas or principles by which they lead their lives. The expression usually goes something like this: "We have been doing it this way for our entire lives." Or, "It is hard to change how we do this." When people react this way to the idea of change, it generally means that they have not taken the time to reevaluate the premise at hand in light of the change of context in their lives. They need to realize that changing the principle or premise is not necessary. Rather, they should strive to apply that principle to a new set of facts and allow the transformation to take place. In doing so, the balance in the relationship might shift and thus allow for a recalibration.

The three marital vignettes illustrated in this chapter exemplify the various ways therapists or consultants can stimulate safe conversations with couples, helping them gain access to the meanings behind their patterns of behavior and facilitating the change process as a result. These methods can be used at various points in a professional's work with a couple, although they are often more useful during the natural transitions that couples have to make throughout their life cycle together. Educating and empowering couples to use these tools allows them to review together in a thoughtful way the meaning and motivation that informs their decision making.

Chapter 4

Parents of Children through Age 20

Although money is a constant reality in family life, it remains a difficult subject for most parents to address with their children. For some, talking to young children about money seems premature and generally unnecessary. Even those parents who have learned to be transparent about many other subjects are at a loss when it comes to the money conversation, stymied by the challenge it presents. Despite the awkwardness and secrecy often associated with the subject, parents need to learn how to approach money issues with their children. Teaching our kids about money and developing their financial skills gives them tools to build a stronger sense of self as well as a moral compass that guides them toward resilience and independence.

Becoming a parent is irrevocable, a role acquired forever with the birth or adoption of a child. But whereas being a parent is a constant, the parenting experience shifts depending on the child's age and the context of the family, and requires balancing many competing agendas. The responsibility of parenting is great; the challenges can be overwhelming. Until recently, our own parents were the only ones available to teach us when we became parents ourselves. Today, there are numerous resources to educate parents, including books, seminars, and the Internet. But the focus for most of these resources is primarily the years from birth through adolescence. Guidance for parenting older children—college age and beyond—is less common. With the longevity and mobility inherent in the twenty-first century, these later stages of family relationships are becoming more demanding because parents live longer and families continue to spread out geographically. As a result, avoidance of money conversations is the path most parents take.

Money and financial independence are key issues for parenting throughout childhood and adulthood. Using money talk as a tool toward functional independence, and linking money and values, will help deepen these intergenerational conversations at whatever stage of life.

In this chapter, we focus on parenting during the childhood years and include the application of our methodology to four family cases, each at a different stage of the family's life cycle. During the child-rearing years, the most common issues relating to money are allowance, philanthropy, and work.

Parents and teachers generally use age-appropriate methods to teach children how to make simple decisions. A parent might ask a five-year-old to choose between two activities and guide the youngster through the decision process, but not give a choice about bedtime. Children who learn how to make decisions during childhood become adults with capacity for self-determination, responsibility, and accountability that enhance a built-in resilience.

Children internalize values through multiple avenues. First and foremost, children watch what their parents do more closely than they listen to what their parents say, absorbing their parents' values by observation. Parents serve as children's primary role models, and the old motto "do as I say, not as I do" can confuse them. If there is underground tension between the parents, children have a more difficult time understanding the desired message. As their value system evolves, the core of their identity gets stronger and becomes a guide for life. Values then become the internal compass, the foundation for character.

The challenge for parents is to remain conscious of their own values, and to link them to their actions, daily activities, and conversations with their children. Parents who carefully think through and articulate the values they care most deeply about raise children in harmony with those values. Parents who value work and education will guide their children through their early years with actions and activities that highlight these priorities. The anticipated result is to raise children who will make life and career choices that are grounded in those values. Parents who value wealth, social status, material possessions, and competition above all else will raise children who struggle with the purpose of their lives.

Although the historical tendency in child rearing has been to avoid talking about money as it relates to values, it is important to do exactly that. Linking values to money accomplishes three objectives for families: (1) it enhances the values-promotion agenda by making what might have been unconscious or intuitive more conscious, (2) it provides a language for open communication about money, and (3) it sets a format for teaching a decision-making process.

The vignettes in this chapter examine how values promotion linked to money can benefit parenting at four stages of a child's social and emotional development. Three themes are natural points of entry and connection for children: allowance, philanthropy, and work. Each case centers around one or two of these themes. These examples highlight the *what* and the *how* of the connections between money and values. The emphasis is on the value linkage and how the connection with money informs the parenting agenda and resolves specific dilemmas. Multiple examples are addressed within the relational context. For professionals deciding to promote this methodology, these ideas and examples reflect principle and practice. They help professionals think about ways to influence clients who want to enhance their family life by integrating a values-based approach to decision making.

Awareness in Families with Preschool Children

Case Study: Valerie Breaks the Silent Code of Money to Manage Tanya's Tantrums

Valerie was constantly complaining to Neil, her husband, about her difficulty in curbing their four-year-old daughter's appetite
(continued)

for toys. No matter what store Valerie walked into, Tanya proceeded to whine and cry incessantly and push Valerie into buying her something. Often Valerie gave in to Tanya's crying because she did not know how else to stop it and was embarrassed by the public display. Neil, who did not understand why Valerie was upset, suggested she take Tanya out of the store or simply buy the toy, but Valerie did not believe that either choice would resolve the issue. Finally, Valerie decided to get some help, and chose to attend a parenting workshop on the subject of money and children. She was so impressed by what she learned, she asked Neil to join her for a private session with the facilitator.

What had surfaced for Valerie at the workshop was her inability to know how to talk about money to her children. She had no memory of money talk in her own family. She realized that the absence of such a discussion had been a disservice to her, and was determined to find a better way to handle this in her own family. The linkage of money and values resonated for her. At the workshop, Valerie had done the card sort exercise to determine core values, and she wanted Neil to do this exercise with her.

Awareness of parents' core values is extremely useful in guiding them as they begin to make the linkage between money and values. It gives consistency to their communication with each other and highlights the tensions—the ambivalence and contradictions—that exist in their individual relationships to money. It gives couples the ability to agree to disagree. It provides the tools to distinguish between solving problems and managing dilemmas. In all these ways, the card sort can lead to smoother parenting and healthier family functioning.

Valerie had already done the card sort at the seminar and was familiar with the exercise. Initially, Neil struggled with it, but as he warmed to the work, he became eager to share his four core values and hear about Valerie's. Neither one was surprised to see their overlap. They recalled talking about these ideas while courting.

They realized that life had become so hectic with their multiple responsibilities of family and work that these discussions about values had dropped off their radar screen. Doing the card sort brought them back to their two shared values, relationship and work, the basis for their mutual desire to share a life together. Neil's other two choices were economics and ethical values. Valerie's were public service and spirituality.

Their interest in one another's choices led to the kind of meaningful conversation that they had rarely found time for since they had become parents. They were curious about where the next step would lead, not understanding how recognizing their values could help Valerie solve her problem with Tanya. Valerie reiterated her concern about her daughter's temper tantrums in toy stores. The facilitator acknowledged the problem and suggested a linkage between Valerie's inability to say no to her daughter and her own financial decision making. Both Valerie and Neil looked puzzled by this and sought clarification.

First, Valerie had to determine how she might use these incidents as opportunities for teaching her daughter and what exactly it was that she wanted to teach. With reflection, Valerie realized that she needed to begin to teach her daughter the distinction between "want" and "need." Next, she could use the opportunity to teach Tanya about money and how to make choices based on priorities. Even at Tanya's age, there were concepts Valerie could introduce into their interactions.

With this clarification, Valerie was better able to think about how to set limits inside or outside their home. She understood that money was not a word to be avoided. It had to be a subject just like any other that she talked about with Tanya. Before Valerie's exposure to our technique, she had thought that Tanya was too young for discussions about money. Valerie's parents had kept her in the dark about money until she had been well into her young adult years. They had never referenced it in any conversations and, as a result, Valerie was confused about integrating money into her own parenting.

Treating money as a taboo subject around children leads to confusion, mystification, and bewilderment. Children observe their parents handling money and talking about money daily. The challenge for parents is *how* to talk to children about money, not *whether* to do so at all. When parents portray a comfort and ease with the topic, it opens the conversation and counters the mystique, allowing time for reflective thought and conversation.

Valerie left the session with new ideas about how to talk to Tanya about money, and she was determined to try them. She was apprehensive, but convinced that making the connection between money and values would work for her. She also began to understand how her internal confusion and inability to address the money topic influenced Tanya's reactions in public. She recognized how much her parents' silence around money had contributed to her own paralysis around the subject. She wanted to change that, hoping to integrate money talk into their lives naturally and comfortably. She even had a specific idea for an activity that would involve collecting money and giving back. Tanya had heard about the Tsunami in the Far East. Valerie had given her just the slightest description of what had happened. Tanya had been upset for all the children affected by the disaster. Valerie decided that they should have a bake sale and raise money to buy some toys for the Tsunami victims. This activity would give the family a chance to reflect on their values and send a clear message about helping others who were less fortunate.

Neil liked Valerie's idea and said he would help organize it. Valerie's ease with this plan informed her that she was definitely on the right path. She was starting to shift the premise for Tanya from need to want, from expectation to appreciation. She realized that this was her responsibility as a parent. Creating these linkages to money situations were ways that Valerie broke the silent code of money for herself and for her daughter.

People generally avoid an issue or become paralyzed around a topic that is fraught with tension for them. In speaking to a therapist, they will frequently detour a conversation so that they end up discussing something other than the subject at hand. If the professional can disentangle the conversation, the connections of meaning can prove to be challenging and liberating for the client. Moreover, creating such pathways for clients is often rewarding for the therapist or coach as well. This is as true for the topic of money as for any other subject.

Implementation in Families with School-Age Children

Case Study: Sonia and Raphael Finally Agree on How to Use Allowance

Sonia and Raphael constantly argued about whether to give their children, aged 9 and 10, an allowance. Raphael wanted to teach their children financial responsibility and sound decision making and thought that an allowance would be the best vehicle to accomplish his goal. Sonia thought an allowance was unnecessary, because teaching their children money management was not a priority for her.

Raphael's motivation came from personal experience. Many years ago, he had overextended his credit card, could not pay his debt, and had to declare bankruptcy, a difficult decision fraught with shame, guilt, and torment. He wanted to teach his kids what he had never learned as a child—financial responsibility and money management. Sonia, never having confronted anything comparable, did not understand. Growing up, her parents had been the providers and decision makers, and now in her marriage, Raphael was playing that role. She assumed her children would follow the same path. Even though she had always worked, she had no problem adding her money to the family money pool.

Dropping the children off at school one morning, Raphael noticed a sign advertising a workshop on allowance and children. He made note of the date and decided then and there that both he and Sonia would attend. He felt committed to resolving the conflict and thought that the workshop might be the ideal opportunity.

At the workshop, the speaker's opening line referred to allowance as a "big family troublemaker" because of the lack of clarity about the objectives for parents and children. She continued by suggesting that allowance be seen as a tool for teaching children values and money management. Although the choice to link values to money is complex, the speaker noted that if parents choose to use allowance as a tool, the first and most important step is to clarify the objective. She defined possible guidelines parents could set to better communicate with their children. These included the basic concepts of money management: counting, saving, sharing, growing, and spending. She further identified allowance as a values-based tool for teaching aspects of spending, saving, and sharing, and suggested that this conversation become ongoing in the format of a regular family meeting. Her message to the parents was succinct: tell your children that you intend to use an allowance to teach them how to save and spend wisely, based on a set of priorities that you will help them develop.

Sonia responded to the speaker's suggestions with skepticism. She turned to Raphael and said that she had not learned about values this way and couldn't imagine doing this with their kids. Raphael replied that the way their parents had raised them differed in many aspects from their own child-rearing ideas. He wondered why change was such a hurdle for Sonia, knowing as he did how she felt about money. He acknowledged how hard she worked both at home and at her workplace, and commented that she was definitely a role model for their kids. Why then was she balking at this allowance issue?

For many people, the pattern set for them in childhood is internalized and remains their guide throughout life. They often find it impossible to conceive changing these patterns or their underlying premises. This resistance might not seem relevant to the issue, but in exploring family patterns, the logjam opens, and clients learn that their patterns run very deeply in their inner lives.

As the seminar continued, the speaker introduced an idea that neither Sonia nor Raphael had ever considered. She presented the process values card sort and asked Sonia and Raphael to sort the cards to describe the process they used to make financial decisions in their families.

Sonia chose hierarchy, exclusive values, and transparency. She quickly saw that although she had always been a contributor to the family financial pool, she had never been a decision maker and was continuing the same pattern with which she had been raised.

Although she had talked about women making and having choices, she realized at that moment how much the patriarchal culture of her roots had influenced her. She was confronted with her own contradiction; her perception of independence alongside her dependence on the men in her life to make financial decisions. As she considered all this new information, she began to connect her reluctance to give her children an allowance and teach them money management skills with her reluctance to break that pattern. Could she do for them what she had not done for herself? She began to reflect on the implications of this discrepancy for herself and her family, recognizing that a part of her wanted to change and another part preferred having Raphael make those decisions. Her personal conflict was situated between her sense of financial responsibility and her inherent desire for continued dependency. Was financial dependence the only way she knew how to show her emotional connectedness to the men in her life? Could she possibly be financially independent and still maintain her attachment to Raphael?

It is important to confront the contradictions within ourselves as well as the contradictions we experience with others. Addressing the messiness of these tensions allows people to explore ambivalences that are often subconscious, leading them to a deeper understanding of the issues and guiding them to resolution.

Walking out of the workshop, Sonia suggested to Raphael that they continue the conversation about allowance and their children. She thanked him for suggesting they attend the workshop and noted that she needed some time to think about all the ramifications for her before they could talk.

Sonia's new consciousness of her underlying familial and cultural influences had resounded for her as she sorted the process cards. Although she thought that she had overcome her patriarchic roots, she immediately understood the inherent discrepancy. Raphael was not standing in her way. She was! She wanted her children to grow up with decision-making prowess, something she had never had, yet she had consistently resisted Raphael's suggestion to give them the tools to do so. Now she understood why. Her inner tension had to do with her desire to make her own decisions and yet maintain her long-term dependence on the man of the house. She definitely did not want her children to face the same dilemmas. She knew she would have to change and that the allowance could be a first step in that direction.

The process of change starts with the desire to do something differently. The recognition of this desire is a good first step, but the challenge then becomes implementing the new behavior. Undoubtedly, the old premises will lurk in the shadows and surface, but acknowledging the conflicting premises in the first place is the biggest hurdle.

Over the next few weeks, Sonia and Raphael talked about giving their children an allowance. They clarified their objectives together, set a course of action, and even incorporated the value of charity into their plan. They defined the three teaching objectives as saving, spending, and giving. The saving and spending would be based on each child's defined reality and desires. The giving would become a family experience. They would start a *philanthropy jar* and request that each week the children contribute some of their allowance to the jar. They would add their own loose change to the jar, thus making it a cooperative family activity. Every six months, at one of their family meetings, they would all decide what to do with the accumulated money in the jar.

Sonia felt good about their plan for allowance, appreciating it as a tool. Raphael was thrilled to teach his children values-based money management. Sonia especially liked the added dimension of the philanthropy jar. She acknowledged that this was a big change from anything she had ever experienced with money in her childhood, having never had to learn how to make these decisions. But it all felt right to her, and she thanked Raphael for pushing her on this issue. She knew that she and her family would have useful learning experiences from this new plan.

Guiding parents to conscious awareness of both content and process values often leads to an insightful moment. Although most people live their values intuitively, it is the consciousness and recognition of how the values inform our thoughts, actions, and feelings that prod people to either use them more deliberately or change them. Focusing on financial decision making often provides multiple opportunities for discussion and collaboration within the family's life experience, especially when the process is tracked through generations.

Managing Dilemmas in Families with Adolescent Children

Case Study: Yvette and Albert Resolve the Complication of Money in Their Blended Family

Yvette and Albert have been married for 10 years and between them have four children ranging in age from 12 to 17. The oldest two children are Albert's children with his first wife, who died. The two younger children are Yvette's children from her first marriage, which ended in divorce, and these children also spend quality time with their natural father. Yvette and Albert were embroiled in an ongoing debate about whether to have their children work after school or take summer jobs. Yvette went back and forth on this issue. When she spoke with her ex-husband, she agreed with him that the children did not need any more pressure or responsibility, since their days were already filled with both academics and athletics. Albert felt that the children should be encouraged to work. Yvette could see both perspectives but was caught between the differing opinions of Albert and her ex-husband. Albert felt very strongly that his children should learn "how to be in the world" by taking on the responsibilities of work and reporting to a boss. He had a clear perspective on how this should happen, having worked from the time he was nine, and he wanted his children to have the same experience. Yvette and Albert argued constantly about this, and finally agreed to see a professional who could help them resolve the problem.

Remarriage brings with it special complexities. The subject of money and financial responsibility is fraught with multiple meanings and tensions in general, but especially in blended families. In many situations, operating assumptions from one's family of origin as well as from a first marriage come into conflict. In addition, the multiple parents, with their inherent differences, can be confusing or open to manipulation by and for the children.

During the consultation, Yvette and Albert were asked to do the content values card sort. They discovered that they agreed on many of the same values, including work. They went on to use the process values card sort and again found many points of agreement. They turned to the therapist with a questioning look. "Why are we arguing?" they asked. "If you say using values is such a good road map and we are so in sync, why are we arguing so much?"

In exploring the issues with Yvette and Albert, it became clear that the problem related to neither money nor values. Yvette's ambivalence was connected to the impact of this decision on her family relationships. What would happen if there was a fundamental inconsistency within their family? How would this impact their family dynamic? They all lived together and had struggled to create a good family environment. Yvette was concerned that this disagreement would cause a rift between her children and Albert's, and as a result, the children would lose that unified feeling that they, as parents, had worked so hard to create. She did not know how to explain this discrepancy to the children, and she was concerned about how her alignment with her ex-husband would affect both Albert and the children.

When couples explore the meaning of their values, they sometimes discover that although they agree on basic values, they disagree about how to implement them. Teasing out that disagreement to discuss and resolve it is crucial for the family. One resolution is to agree to disagree openly, thus eliminating tension, negative undercurrents, and splits in the family dynamic. When couples agree to disagree, the conversation that was once potentially fraught with conflict becomes more civil, with respect and tolerance for difference. Managing dilemmas like these with transparency is always better than maintaining underground hidden agendas.

Yvette and Albert came to realize that they could treat the issue of working differently for their children. Albert could inculcate his version of the work value by expecting his children to have after-school jobs, while Yvette need not have that expectation of her children. Open communication with the four children about this issue was an important dimension of their plan to "agree to disagree." Because they chose this resolution, Albert and Yvette knew that numerous discrepancies would surface, and that they would have to be prepared to discuss them with clarity. They would have to explain to their children that sometimes similar values can be expressed differently.

Because Yvette and Albert still wanted to teach their children about money, beyond the realm of working, they decided to hold a series of family meetings to plan a family vacation. They would give the children some defining boundaries, but together they would sort out the planning process with a budget and set of priorities. This activity would foster the family cohesiveness that worried Yvette. At the same time, it would become a venue for teaching their children how to create priorities and budget their funds.

Yvette and Albert learned that financial competency, whether it is achieved through working after-school jobs or learning how to maintain a budget, is a vehicle for kids to manifest their values and their character. It also demonstrates self-reliance and discipline, acknowledging who they are and who they will become. Literacy in the money space matters. Learning how to communicate, understand, and use the basic ideas and mechanisms of our capitalistic culture adds a significant dimension to children's development, giving them a sense of independence and autonomy.

Transformation in Families with College-Age Children

Case Study: Karen Responds to Tragedy and Grace Fills with Pride

Karen, a freshman at the University of Pennsylvania, was sitting in her morning class on September 11, 2001, when someone ran in to tell them about the planes crashing into the Twin Towers in New York. Initially, Karen could not make sense of the news. She stared in disbelief, her shock palpable. Karen's mother, Grace, worked at the World Trade Center. She bolted back to her dorm room to call her mother, and when she could not get through by phone, she gathered her things and ran to the train station, needing to get home to make sure her mom was safe.

(continued)

When she finally made it home, Karen discovered that her mother had not gone to work that day because she had been sick. Karen's relief was immediate and she could not stop crying and hugging her mom. Later, sobered by the unfolding news, they sat together watching the television, stunned by all that had happened. Periodically, they turned to one another to hug, grateful for having been spared the fate of so many of Grace's colleagues.

Two days later, Karen went back to school and decided that she had to do something to help families who had not been as blessed as hers. In particular, two families in her neighborhood had lost family members, each suffering great emotional loss and both facing enormous financial hurdles. Karen decided to start her own campaign to raise funds for them, but first she needed to learn how to organize such a campaign.

Luckily, Karen knew that she could put into action what she wanted to do, because over the years her mother had helped her master money management and the alignment of values. She remembered all the fights they had had when her mother insisted on teaching her techniques for managing money, but now she was grateful for it.

Karen and her mother had struggled financially for many years. Ten years earlier, her husband had died, and Grace had to balance work and family responsibilities with little support. She had proudly managed to reach the juncture of Karen's launch to college, but during Karen's childhood, Grace had been conflicted between her need to teach Karen financial responsibility and her desire to make up to Karen for the loss of her father by supplying her with material things. Throughout her high school years, Grace had given Karen an allowance to cover her expenses—even creating a clothing budget—which had sometimes led to tension between them. Karen worked after school to earn extra money when she wanted something she could not afford from her allowance.

Grace's consistency in the money management arena was a result of the parenting group she joined right after her husband's death. That group had discussed the linkage of money and values and even asked the parents to apply that thinking to themselves before they worked with their children. Grace's awareness of how she spent her money guided her to understand more fully how she could teach her daughter these principles. Teaching Karen about money and values had not been easy. She was the kind of kid who wanted everything in sight. If her friends were wearing a certain sweater, she wanted it, too, and the tension between Karen and her mother was often explosive. Grace worked hard to give her daughter the best of everything, but understood how detrimental "having it all" would have been to Karen. She used the ideas of value linkage and priority setting to educate her daughter. Apparently, it had worked.

When Karen called to tell her mom what she had decided to do, Grace was speechless, her heart filling with pride. Karen had made this decision without ever discussing it with Grace and had mastered what to do and how to do it. She had laid the plans for developing the fund-raising campaign at her school, and had already collected funds from the students in her dorm. Grace was stunned by her daughter's ability to apply her values and skills to this project, and she loved that Karen had taken her idea one step further into the dimension of philan-thropy. Grace understood that Karen's values and character were reflected in this project and that her ability to implement was the result of all that Grace had taught her daughter over the years.

Internalization of values takes place over time. The process is never direct and instantaneous, and the transformation is unique to each individual, manifesting itself in various actions. The thought processes described in this book create a matrix that informs behavior. The transmission of our values and their linkage to money leads to the development of strong, independent individuals, the "human capital" of the family.

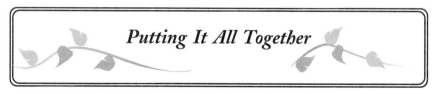

Putting It All Together

In parenting children through adolescence and young adulthood, it is advisable to be as consistent as possible with the handling of money. Linking values to money builds that foundation and creates a language to address the discrepancies. The case vignettes presented in this chapter highlight this premise. In each case it was important for the parent to clarify the underlying premise connected to the meaning of money.

Marcia is better able to deal with Tanya's desires and frustrations when she herself makes the linkage and appreciates the obstacles of her own personal assumptions. Sonia and Raphael surpass their hurdle around allowance by opening the conversation. Albert and Yvette manage their family discrepancies around work through widening their lens and addressing the family culture. Lastly, Grace fills with pride when her 18-year-old daughter Karen assumes responsibility and seeks a philanthropic initiative independently after observing a tragedy.

In each scenario, the path was cleared for the teaching and development of money management and decision-making skills. In raising children, it is important to attend to these parallel tracks. Using values as the linkage provides an expanded and neutral language. Raising children in the twenty-first century presents multiple challenges. Teaching them about money and meaning provides a foundation for their development.

Chapter 5

Parents of Children 21 and Older

This chapter, presented from a parental perspective, focuses on parenting older children with the application of our method- ology to four age-related cases. The themes that recur during these later stages of parenting relate to work, philanthropy, and accumulation or transfer of assets. Tension surfaces for parents as they reorient and redefine their relationships with their children. The continuum of caretaking, independence, and interdependence becomes more fluid and requires a reassessment of the emotional connections as a grown child becomes self-directed and self-supporting, shaping his or her own life. The parent-child relationship shifts from one of dependency in early life to one of mutuality in later years. This shift involves parents learning to see their children as adults functioning in the world, and children coming to think of their parents as people with a history, life, and concerns of their own. When money serves as a substitute for the connection and represents control and power, family relationships become dysfunctional. Having a long-term perspective on parenting requires the appreciation of the vicissitudes of the parent-child connection on the continuum of caretaking to interdependence with empowerment as the under- lying theme. The role of money and financial responsibility features prominently in such a long-term parenting plan.

Richard came to see me for what he called his "check-in," since our professional connection had transformed over the years into a coaching relationship. At the beginning of our session, I asked about his children, who were now grown and ranged in age from 21 to 27. Richard smiled proudly at me and reported that their third child had just been married and that he considered "Number One," as he called his oldest child, successfully launched. Three of his five children were married, so I wondered why only one of them was considered launched in his father's eyes. Richard explained that he had set three criteria for the launching of his children into adulthood: family life shaped, career path determined, and financial independence reached. Apparently, his oldest child had recently completed all three goals.

Self-sufficiency and self-resilience become key objectives for grown children. Because the most prominent tension for adults in our culture is between their economic and practical needs, on the one hand, and their relationships on the other, this dynamic forms the lens through which we parent our adult children. The challenge is to calibrate the support we give our children as they make their way in the world. The path leading to their ultimate independence can be bumpy, and so keeping the line of communication open is important. Acting as a sounding board, without providing solutions allows parents to exert influence and give their children feedback. Trying to solve problems for them or teach them lessons by providing money can backfire. Using the values and money linkage at this stage of the parenting journey helps families work out some of the contradictory and normal potentially difficult issues that surface during the early developmental phases of the adult life cycle.

In a *Generation to Generation: Life Cycles of the Family Business*, Kelin Gersick et al. refer to Daniel Levinson's model as "phases of transition and stability that continue throughout an adult's life." Gersick uses the metaphor of building and rebuilding one's house to describe the task of adults as they move through their lives. In the early adult years, the task is to construct those boundaries that provide stability for independence. As adults expand their lives through relationships and careers, they make transitions and rebuild the house using past experiences to create the new stability.

The transition of the adult child requires a shift of the parents as well, a dynamic process as their adult children change their primary relationship from their family of origin to the next phase, which might be forming a nuclear family or designing a life as a single adult.

Awareness in Families with Children in Their Twenties

Case Study: Fran Launches Scott

Fran came to talk to me about her 23-year-old son, Scott, who had recently graduated from college and started his first job. Although his parents rarely saw him, Scott's impact was keenly felt in the family home. Fran's major concern was that Scott seemed to be spending money without responsibility. She and her husband, Herb, had always given him carte blanche with money, never setting boundaries around spending, and she understood now the consequences of that policy as she uttered in despair, "We made such a mistake!" She knew something had to change, and had come to talk about how to begin.

Rather than attempt to teach children about money management, parents too often take the easier route of issuing their kids funds according to perceived need. Some parents give their children everything in the service of protection, with material satiation taking the place of emotional nurturance. At every stage of life, it takes effort to teach children the skills required to manage money. Teaching children to follow a budget requires thought and practice, but parents who do so end up with adults who respect and care about their future. Fran and Herb had not done this with Scott when he was younger, and they wanted to know if it was too late to begin, now that he was in his twenties.

Listening to Fran, I noted that her concerns centered on the lack of discretion that Scott showed in his spending patterns. He would go out to dinner with friends and pay for everyone using his credit card. When shopping, he would invariably buy the latest designer fad. And, his cell phone bill was off the charts. Although he had started working, he was not paying for any of these expenses with his own money. Fran queried what exactly her son was spending his money on, fearing he did not understand that, as a working adult, he had assumed financial responsibility. Where had they gone wrong?

Throughout the years, Fran and Herb's primary parenting difficulty had always been setting limits for their children. A dual-career couple, they could be described as a loving family with core values of work, education, relationship, and philanthropy. The values discussion was not a new one for them, but Fran's dilemma was how to introduce and manage a financial discussion with her son. She had avoided approaching Scott about all these issues, fearing that she would become enraged and sabotage any possibility for real conversation. She understood that her anger, focused as it was on Scott's behavior, was also related to her disappointment in herself as a parent.

The first step in neutralizing her anger was to help Fran frame the conversation she would have with Scott. I handed her the content values cards and suggested that she find the three or four cards that were motivating her toward this decision to teach Scott budgeting to curb his excessive expenses. She immediately chose financial responsibility, economics, and material possessions.

Fran was pleased to have the language she needed to frame the anticipated conversation and to defuse some of her anger and frustration. She had been paralyzed by her emotional response to Scott's behavior, bewildered by his failure to take more financial responsibility when he was so responsible in many other ways. She understood that the time had come to change the family's financial rules.

It is never too late to mentor children financially. The key fact that parents with adult children in their twenties need to remember is that just because something has not happened to date doesn't mean that it can't happen now. Parenting is a complicated task, and seizing opportunities to rework the gaps is not only permissible but advisable and healthy. The challenge is in choosing the correct stance. Articulating the desire to be a resource to a child at this age can enhance the child's trajectory toward independence and resilience.

With the understanding and clarity she gained in the content values card sort exercise, Fran looked quizzically at me, seeking advice about the "how to" of her implementation. This time, I handed her the process cards. She looked at the cards and smiled, quickly understanding my point.

Fran chose three cards: "empowerment," "collaboration," and "transparency." We reviewed what these values meant to her. When Scott's spending went out of control, Fran had responded by "plugging the hole in the money dike." Although she realized that hierarchical tactic was likely to turn Scott away from a discussion with her, she reiterated her desire to sit with Scott, develop a budget with him, and help him learn to live within realistic financial constraints. She acknowledged the tension that was bound to be present, and took responsibility for this void in their parenting.

Herb, meanwhile, was not present at this session. His idea had been to sit down and read Scott the "riot act." Although Fran agreed with the desired outcome, she did not agree with Herb's proposed tactic, afraid it would produce only anger and bitter resentment. That was her primary reason for calling me, and now she was pleased to have a manageable plan of action. She was ready to go home, talk with Herb, and then sit down with Scott.

A person can be more effective at communicating with others by connecting the issue to its relevant emotion or internal conflict and distinguishing personal disappointments and frustrations from those of the other party. It is possible to neutralize the intensity of affect by being clear about these perspectives. The structure of safe language can provide the trust it takes to get to the multiple meanings that elude people in more difficult conversations, guiding them toward those meanings and neutralizing the underlying affect.

Implementation in Families with Children Aged Thirty and Above

Case Study: The Group's Input Helps Harold

At the last session of the Parenting Forum at the Ackerman Institute, Harold was ready to talk to the group about a disturbing incident that had happened with his 38-year-old son Mark. The group had formed to explore money issues that arose when parenting adult children. This third session was

(continued)

focused on the application of the money and values linkage to personal experiences.

As Harold began his presentation, he bemoaned the incident, asserting that he did not understand where he had gone wrong. Mark and his wife Myra had recently purchased a three-bedroom home. Harold had been thrilled when his son and daughter-in-law had found the apartment and had offered to pay for the down payment with no strings attached. With the sale of a premarital apartment, this gift from Harold, and a mortgage, Mark and his wife were able to purchase the apartment. They had been very grateful to Harold for his generosity.

Omitted in their calculations, however, were the costs of renovation required for move-in. Mark had gone back to Harold to ask for a loan. This time, Harold thought a structured loan would be appropriate. In his desire to teach his son about financial responsibility, Harold proposed a deal whereby he would loan them the money at 2 percent above prime, defer interest for a year, take a balloon repayment of the interest after two years, and ask for the apartment as collateral. Mark did not react to this plan, but Myra became enraged at the proposal, which she perceived as harsh for a family loan. Mark felt trapped between his wife and father and had subsequently turned down Harold's offer. Harold was surprised by the rejection and did not understand the tension that he had created between the couple. He thought he was being collaborative and empowering, according to his understanding of the process values cards.

In guiding adult children (usually in their 30s and 40s) through the transition of establishing a home, parents have to decide if and how they can be a resource to their children. In some situations, serving as a resource might simply mean providing them the wisdom of experience. In others, it might be loaning or gifting monies for a down payment or purchase. In either situation, it is crucial for parents to remain, like a coach, on the sidelines until needed, while the children experience choosing, purchasing, and financing their first asset. For the parent, this process can reflect their child's transition from dependence to independence. Parents can be guided through this transition with the process values cards. Applying them to a specific situation—such as the child's first home purchase—is helpful for most people.

Harold thought that gifting Mark and Myra the down payment funds was an act of collaboration, and he did not understand that his children perceived the same actions as high-handed. The Ackerman group agreed that all the initial steps (looking at the apartment with them and offering the money in the first place) had been collaborative to a degree. They queried Harold about the conversations he had with Mark around the purchase and financing of the apartment. Harold noted that most of those conversations had been informational rather than advisory.

Jane, another member of the Ackerman group, tried to be helpful by telling the story of her daughter who had also recently purchased an apartment. She described the process with her daughter as a collaborative one that she created by positioning herself as a sounding board while her daughter looked for, chose, and purchased the apartment. Mother and daughter talked and strategized together about interviews, financing options, and every other step of the procedure. Harold confessed to the group that he had not been involved in that way. He and Mark had not experienced the nuanced discussions that Jane described, even though Harold knew that Mark had experienced many of the same anxieties as Jane's daughter.

In the implementation phase, the application of process values can be tricky, especially if the objective is to change an old pattern. Some parents continue to make hierarchical decisions for their adult children, not recognizing the tension inherent in that old form of attachment. As the young adult moves toward more independent functioning, navigating that tension becomes the challenge for the parent. The process values card sort can be a helpful tool in identifying the desired stance for this transition. There are inevitable contradictions between what a person wants to do and how these intentions are implemented, but the important and difficult step is to bring those discrepancies to the surface so that families can talk about them.

Harold had envisioned becoming a resource for his son in two ways: he wanted to help financially, and he wanted to use the renovation loan to teach Mark financial responsibility. As was his pattern, however, Harold had not discussed this issue with anyone. He had decided what he would propose without ever having discussed it with Mark. In addition to the ingrained pattern that kept Harold from discussing the terms and implications of the loan, he was also fearful that Mark would begin to see him as an open pocketbook and take advantage of that position. This fear was so powerful that it overshadowed his commitment to teach financial responsibility to Mark in an empowering, collaborative manner. Despite Harold's real concern for his son's well-being, there had been no collaborative effort around the loan issue.

The tension between a parent's obligation to encourage their child's independence and the desire to be supportive and to function as a resource becomes a significant obstacle course for some families with adult children. Harold's fear of being taken advantage of, a personal issue for him, complicated the implications of this situation, making it hard to sort through its multilayered meanings. When the stance of the parent shifts to a collaborative one, like the position Jane took, the conversation between parent and adult child can begin to transform to one of mutuality and respect. Although Harold had identified "collaboration" as a process value, the meaning of that value for him contradicted others' understanding.

Using the card sort as a frame of reference, clients can explore the meaning of their actions and distinguish between an internal conversation and the actual action. Group conversations like the one Harold experienced in the Ackerman project, can support the effort to make these distinctions. Sometimes, the way a parent chooses to implement a decision is not always in concert with that parent's perceived ideal, and in such situations, conversations that include the reactions of others can help a parent to align thought and action.

Managing Dilemmas in Families with Children in Their Forties

Case Study: Leon Confronts the Complexities of Loss and Family

Leon's wife, Carrie, passed away suddenly and unexpectedly, and the shock had reverberated throughout the family. It had been a second marriage for both of them, a blended family of children from each of their previous marriages that had lasted 28 years. Family relationships had always been a key focus for Leon and Carrie. When Leon called me for a consult, he was looking for someone who would listen to his thought process and guide him through the onslaught of multiple competing emotions.

When death occurs in a family, the emotional upheaval is great, and the loss affects everyone in the family unit. The practical and emotional ramifications to every tragic event encompass both money and relationships, and it is difficult for most families to manage them. Initially, the shock and grief surface, although sometimes people will allow the practical agenda to overshadow their grief as a coping mechanism. Families are unique, and therefore each situation brings with it the diverse issues and emotions of its members. Because of the range of perspectives in any given family, many dilemmas surface during the decision-making process following a death, and the seesaw between the emotional process and the practical action can become challenging. Values can serve as a foundational force during this time of upheaval.

Leon's children, who were in their forties and had children of their own, were stunned and saddened by Carrie's death. They had grown to love and embrace her as their father's wife, a good friend, and confidante. Their grief was naturally focused on the meaning of that loss for them and their concern for their father and his future life without Carrie. How would he manage alone? Meanwhile, Carrie's children were both grief stricken and traumatized. They had been a closely knit family after their parents divorced, and they relied on their mother for many things. Their loss was so profound that they could not begin to imagine life without her. Moreover, she had always been the link between them and Leon, and so their future relationship to him seemed unclear.

Leon was devastated by this sudden trauma and felt emotionally unhinged. His initial reaction was to take action to ease his pain. He decided that what might comfort him would be to remove all signs of Carrie, and he did this by removing photographs, cleaning out her closet and packing up all her papers. After getting through the memorial service, he immediately set up meetings with his estate lawyer, and asked that Carrie's children attend those meetings. For Leon, taking action on all fronts became his way of coping with the pain of his loss.

Carrie's children were stunned by his behavior. They could barely get through the funeral and first weeks of mourning for the mother who had been such an integral part of each of their lives. They appreciated Leon's loss and wanted to comfort him, but somehow their paths diverged. Leon recognized what was happening and felt that their separate paths had become a betrayal of Carrie, whose mission had always been to keep the family bonded. He wanted to reassure Carrie's children that he was there for them, but he was anxious, as well, to begin dealing with her estate issues and to assure them financial security. He addressed these issues with Carrie's children and could immediately sense their retreat from him, which made him feel even more uncomfortable, since he did not want to harm the connection he had with them.

When a death like Carrie's occurs, the family is called on to adapt to the loss. Immediate and long-term processes are triggered as the family begins to reorganize and accept the loss. Adaptation in this sense means finding ways to put the loss in perspective and move on with life. This is reflected in emotional, practical, and financial dimensions. There is no set timetable or sequencing to this process. It is a mistake to impose expectations of stages, or schedules on such a complex process as grief, given the diversity of family and individual coping styles. In fact, dilemmas often arise around pacing the decisions, where feasible, while honoring the varied emotional processes.

Leon recognized his proclivity toward action as his coping mechanism. We talked about the two parallel processes, emotional and practical, and the problem of pacing. With the content values as my frame of reference, I probed and prodded Leon to identify his most important priority at this time. Leon's quick response was relational. He knew Carrie would want him to ensure the continuity of the family relationships they had spent so much effort fostering. Throughout our conversation, Leon reiterated his desire to maintain his connection with Carrie's children. In response, I underscored his relational priority and pointed to the dissonance between his coping style and his identified priority. I acknowledged his anxiety relating to his future life and the unknown, and I queried him about the timing of dealing with the estate matters. Asking if the probate could wait for a month, I tried to help Leon focus on the relational value as his guidepost in monitoring his action steps. He understood his impulse to wipe out traces of Carrie as a means of coping with his pain, and further understood his desire to get the probate done as originating in the same place.

I suggested he try to vet his actions through a relational lens, which would require him to reflect on how the others in his family might experience his actions. In addition, I asked him to consider shifting his stance with Carrie's adult children by asking them about their thoughts rather than just telling them what his decisions were. He bridled at that suggestion but said he could try. At least he had a frame of reference for himself and Carrie's children that could guide him through the next months. He valued his parenting role and began to appreciate the shift from his traditional hierarchical stance to a more collaborative one.

The upheaval and disorganization that families may experience in the immediate aftermath of a loss like Carrie's may lead some family members to make precipitous moves. The meaning and consequences of the loss vary depending on factors as various as the cause of death, the role of the deceased in the family, money implications, and personal, cultural, and spiritual beliefs. Pacing and sequencing the decision making following a death can be the key to the realignment and reorganization of the family. Accepting the death and using the experience transformationally to reconnect to a life course without this member reinforces a family's resilience.

Transformation in Families with Children Fifty and Older

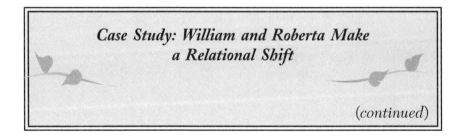

Case Study: William and Roberta Make a Relational Shift

(continued)

For William and Roberta, their life journey had progressed with few big hurdles, and they had just celebrated their fiftieth wedding anniversary. Their two grown children had traveled west to mark the celebration. After that visit, Louise, their older daughter, had started to call them more regularly, checking in to see how they were doing, and then inviting them to come east for a visit. Roberta was reluctant to make the long trip. Travel was not easy for her anymore, but William convinced her that they should make the journey. By the middle of the visit, they understood why their daughters had wanted them to come. The daughters proposed that William and Roberta move back east so that, as a family, they could enjoy each other more.

With today's advances in medicine, people are living longer and families are spanning multiple generations. Family relationships are especially significant throughout later life for most adults, when contact and connection are extremely important. The challenge for parents and children at this later stage of life is the change that takes place in their relationship as the children begin to take care of their parents and the parents gradually lose their independence. When there is no major illness or accident, this transformation may take place gradually over time. In other circumstances, the transition causes a significant strain on everyone in the family. No matter what the circumstance, money can become a central theme.

William had retired late in life, at age 75. He and Roberta had spent most of their time together. Louise and her sister Gwen had realized through telephone contact that their parents were spending most of their time alone in their apartment. Louise also calculated that since her father's retirement, they had less disposable income to use for travel and entertainment. She knew her father would be reluctant to talk about his financial situation, but she and her sister met to discuss what they could do to better their parents' quality of life in these later years.

When the girls offered up their plan to move their parents east, William and Roberta were shocked. How could they leave California? What would they do in New York? It would be cold! How could they maintain their independence? Gwen and Louise proposed that William and Roberta move into an apartment that Louise had purchased. They could afford to pay the maintenance, and Louise would service the debt. The location was near stores for their daily functional living and within walking distance of Louise's home. They could easily access cultural and social activities within the city and get to see their daughters frequently. How could William and Roberta argue with this plan? Their daughters had covered every practical base.

In keeping with the family relational pattern, however, there had been no focus on how anyone really felt about the proposal. William responded positively and was quite comfortable allowing his daughters to take on more responsibility for their life. He was relieved by this anticipated support. Roberta, however, was stuck on the caretaking dimension of the proposal and had a strong reaction to Louise's presentation. She said she needed time to think about it.

From Roberta's perspective, this plan highlighted their emotional and financial dependence on their daughters. Although she had been impressed by their thoroughness, Roberta felt great discomfort with the implication. Was she exaggerating what could happen? Would she and William lose their sense of independence? Would she and William feel "watched over"? How would accepting this plan affect their parental relationship to the girls?

Louise, a client, discussed their plan with me on numerous occasions. The most significant issues addressed in our conversations related to how to convince her parents that this would be a good move for their family. The talks that she and her sister had with their parents always focused on the positive relational implications for all of them. The financial aspect would be a means to that end. Roberta was convinced by this idea and agreed to the move, which has proven to be successful for this family.

Realistic acceptance of strengths and limitations by older adults becomes a challenge when parents face a shift in their relationship to their children. Allowing adult children to assume some responsibility in their parents' lives honors the children's adulthood and speaks to the confidence and respect that a parent has for an adult child's competence. For the adult child, the ability to take responsibility for aging parents and to recognize what they can or cannot do is equally challenging. Parents can feel comforted when their children work together on these issues, seeing their camaraderie as boding well for the future of the family relations. Money is often a central issue for families during these transitions. Connecting the money issue to language and intent that speaks to relational issues can neutralize some inherent tensions. The key issue for most parents in these shifts becomes maintaining their pride and dignity.

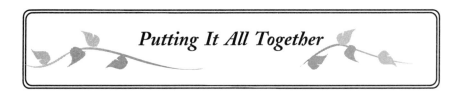

Putting It All Together

Whether parenting young children or adults, money and financial affairs are intertwined in the family life process. The development of resilient and self-sufficient individuals within the family can be enhanced by taking advantage of the opportunities money conversations present. The connection of money and values can be used to tease out the inherent points of tension in a family. Parenting roles and responses shift depending on the age and stage of life of the children as well as the parents. As in the cases of child rearing, parents can use the money and values linkage for transmitting values to their children early in life. And when parenting adult children, the shifting parent-child relationship brings those values into play, affecting major decisions in times of transition.

In this chapter we have seen how the linkage of money and values opened the conversation for Fran and her son Scott. In clarifying the meaning of collaboration with help from the group, Harold was able to change his approach to Mark and Myra. The last two vignettes deal with the shifting nature of parental/child relationships as parents move into their later decades. The ability to traverse the caretaking, independent, and interdependent continuum becomes more of a challenge as parents move into these years.

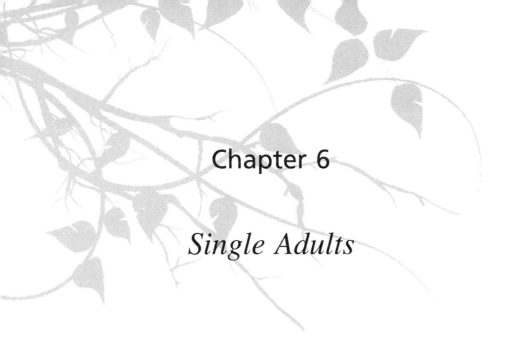

Chapter 6

Single Adults

Living alone, supporting oneself, and planning life as a single adult presents distinctive issues depending on the person's age and life circumstances. The phases of adult development that D. J. Levinson defines as "recycling," "transition," and "stabilization," which incorporate skills, knowledge, and experience from one phase into the next, are useful ways to understand adult lives.

Even though, by definition, a *single adult* is not involved in a formalized or traditional relationship, each of us comes from a family that informs how we think about money and its meaning. That family forms the relational context for an otherwise single adult. Therefore, in working with single adults, whether the focus is launching into independence, acceptance of status, or planning for the future, it is important to think about the meaning of money within the family of origin. Such an analysis can help single adults understand the premises that inform their present attitude.

Connecting money to values and looking at the subject through this relational lens can provide greater insight into past influences and a different format for decision making as adults build, stabilize, and rebuild their lives. For single adults, the opening of the conversation may be the most valuable part of the process because they are not otherwise in consistent dialogue with others on these topics. Advisors, clinicians, or peers who can open these discussions with single adults offer important support for understanding their internal dialogue about money.

The case studies that follow describe the single person's perspective in financial decision making. The situations are age-determined because a single adult's issues shift depending on age and stage of life. As always, the use of the card sort and focused genogram facilitates awareness, supports the adults' implementation of strategies, and guides them toward a transformation of perspective.

Twenties: Awareness

Case Study: Scott's Perspective

In Chapter 5, we met Fran, whose 23-year-old son Scott was living at home. Fran was struggling to find ways to talk to Scott about his need to become more financially responsible. Now imagine the same situation from Scott's perspective.

The atmosphere at home had become quite uncomfortable for everyone, and Scott could not understand what his parents wanted from him. He had started to work at an entry-level job, his first foray into the work world after college. He described the difficulties he was experiencing at his job and with his parents. He did not like the work he was doing nor did he respect the people in his office. At home, his parents were on his back all the time. He felt he had made a bad choice professionally, and he missed his college campus life with the independence it had afforded him. There were times when he even considered going back to school, an unrealistic solution to his discomfort. Eventually, he decided to move into his own apartment.

Although going to college may appear to be the point of adult launching, for many young adults, graduation and the person's first full-time job become the more valid and realistic beginnings of maturation. The financial independence that accompanies work life is the first phase of structuring adult life, enabling the person to leave the family home and to become autonomous. Vacillation between dependency and independence is common during this transition.

Scott went on to describe the tension between him and his parents. They were constantly critical of him, whether it had to do with the mess in his room, the dishes in the sink, or the hour at which he walked through the door at night. He had thought himself beyond all this, too old to be supervised by his parents, and with the constant bickering, life had become unpleasant. He needed to move out, but could not afford his own apartment. He needed help in figuring out how to talk to his parents, who were under a lot of financial stress, about seeking their financial support. They had never talked about financial matters, and Scott did not know where or how to begin.

If money management has not already been a part of family life and discussion, it quickly becomes a reality when children reach adulthood. The steps in creating the structure for life include finding a job, establishing a home, managing a social life, and finding a way to budget for other expenses such as transportation and clothing. These tasks can be done impulsively or reflectively.

In seeking clarification with Scott, I explored the underlying contradiction: the tension between independence and dependence reflected in the conflicts with his parents. He wanted to be treated as an adult, and yet he acted and thought like their kid at home, and certainly they treated him that way. Acknowledging his desire to move to his own place, I asked if he needed their financial support. He responded with alacrity, "Absolutely!" We talked about how he was going to manage this with them and I suggested we use the card sort to clarify his objectives and motivations.

After some hesitation, he decided that financial responsibility was beginning to be important, work was a key issue, and relationships were always on his mind. With these three values highlighted as his primary issues, we had established a structure and a language for conversation. We could then focus our conversation and address Scott's ambivalence around these issues. Scott also articulated his confusion about his parents' point of view because he didn't understand their mixed messages and what seemed to be an abrupt change in their attitude. Sometimes they expected adult behavior, and at other times, they treated him like a child, especially when discussing money. They had never talked about finances with him before; in fact, right through college they had given him funds on an as-needed basis, never holding him accountable for that money. Now they wanted to give him a budget and have him use his own salary for his expenses. This shift in their attitude was confusing for him. How could they expect all this to happen overnight?

The gap between expectations and reality can cause confusion and misunderstanding in families, especially around money issues and particularly when there has been no prior communication about the subject. Identifying the issues and examining multiple perspectives are key to healthier functioning. A conversation between parents and an adult child about money can be informative and enhancing, especially at the launching point.

By the end of our session, Scott was aware of his ambivalence about growing up, in addition to the practical issues he and his parents needed to clarify. His desires to both grow up and be taken care of were constantly at odds, and the interface between his own ambivalence and that of his parents had created tremendous dissonance for them.

Scott suggested they all return together to discuss the tensions that had arisen, claiming that he could have the conversation now that he had spent the time to identify and understand what the tensions were for him and could use the values as a guide for himself.

Thirties: Implementation

Case Study: Carla Makes a Major Financial Decision for Herself

Carla was about to turn 38. She had a great job, lived in New York City and had a wide social network. She was pleased with her career track and the success she had enjoyed. Her lease was up for renewal, and while friends had suggested that she buy an apartment instead of continuing to rent, Carla had rejected this idea out-of-hand as ridiculous. At her mother's suggestion, she had made an appointment to see a financial planner. Leaving that meeting, she found herself surprised by the direction the conversation had taken.

Martha, the financial planner, started the conversation by asking Carla how she envisioned her life in five years' time. She asked about quality-of-life issues rather than financial ones. Carla was taken aback by the direction of the questions. She had anticipated talking numbers. Martha actually handed her a deck of little cards and asked Carla to choose the top four values that would inform the next years of her life.

Carla was surprised by her own choice of "economic," "financial," "relational," and "philanthropic," especially the first two. She would never have articulated them as important areas, but realized how her professional life and personal experiences were influencing these choices. Martha proceeded to query Carla about what these values meant to her, especially the relationship between the value of financial independence and her reluctance to acquire an asset like a home. Carla began to speak about her life circumstances. She had always assumed that she would be married and have children by the time she was 40, and buying a home was part of that vision. She had never pictured herself buying a home as a single person. She was beginning to confront the reality of her single status, and knew she had to consider the financial implications.

For many single women, a career and the desire for family and relationship are a continual dialectic. For some women, the challenge is trying to balance it all. For others, the focus at work prevents them from being available for committed relationships or marriage. For still others, the choice might be to have a child alone. Each set of circumstances brings with it a different set of financial implications. In any case, acknowledging the single status in present and short-term future planning, with a focus on financial planning, is crucial for the long term.

In hearing Carla identify these values, Martha asked her to think about the implications of accepting her single status as her present and near future state. Pondering a moment, Carla responded spontaneously, "I would buy an apartment and create a home for myself!"

She then sat in silence, shocked by her own response. Just two weeks earlier, she had emphatically said "Never!" to that idea. What had just happened, therefore, was so surprising to her that she questioned what had changed. In fact, what had changed was the process Martha had used to focus the conversation, which had worked well for Carla. Rather than putting ideas forward, Martha had asked Carla to choose what was important to her. Carla had picked finance and economics, and this had led her to address her future financial security.

Now that Carla had a firm idea of what she wanted to accomplish financially, she decided to return to talk to Martha further about whether and how she could financially manage buying a home. By the time she returned to Martha's office, Carla was excited about her potential purchase. She wanted to review the numbers and steps required to manage and implement such a purchase. Carla was beginning to feel like a grown up. Martha outlined the tasks for Carla, such as determining her price point within her financial means, calling a broker, purchasing, and financing, all of which sounded simple enough. But when Carla looked at the list, she could feel her anxiety increase. How was she ever going to accomplish this by herself? Who could she talk to for guidance and support while going through these steps? She had never done anything like this before.

Martha took out a second set of cards for Carla to examine—the process values cards. Carla looked at the nine cards and chose "dialogue" and "empowerment" as the two process values most important to her. Carla wanted to do this on her own, but she knew she would need to consult with others as she went through these steps since talking and getting other perspectives were important elements in her decision making. Martha asked Carla whom she planned to consult, and Carla paused, understanding that her choices were limited. Her friends would probably get tired of this conversation, and her mother might simply tell her what to do. Then she thought about her siblings. Perhaps her brother would be a good choice, since he had just purchased his first apartment recently. She hoped that he would not try to tell her what to do the way her mom was always doing.

In a general way, figuring out what process you want and need can help you reach your objective. Identifying her need and then determining what she had to do to satisfy that need became invaluable to Carla as she started her new project. In the past, Carla had intuitively relied on others for consultation as she was working through an issue. This time, she consciously identified and thoughtfully chose those people in her network who would be most helpful.

Most people speak to a trusted advisor, lawyer, accountant, or financial planner when planning a large financial transaction. Carla—and most single people—benefit from such dialogue and consultation. Getting another perspective stimulates the reflective process. For single adults pursuing a financial objective, it can be helpful to determine how and with whom they should consult about the decision.

Ultimately, single adults must make their own decisions, but the processes they use might differ. Financial decision making presents choices and the need to gain knowledge through conversation. It lifts singles out of their internal dialogue and solitary position.

The more Carla thought about it, the more she felt comfortable about consulting with her brother. She decided to call him in a few days, and knowing his first question would be about her price point and ability to make a down payment, she turned to Martha to address that dimension.

When professional advisors work with single adults, talking about values *before* financial choices makes it more likely that the financial tasks will reach completion. Too often, lawyers, accountants, and financial planners encounter a reluctance to complete a task such as signing a will, making an investment decision, or setting up a trust. This indecisiveness usually reflects some unidentified ambivalence for the client. The card sorts help identify the client's key motivators and internal hurdles. These tools provide a vetting process, give meaning to the money conversation, and frequently lead to closure.

Forties: Managing Dilemmas

Case Study: Helen Struggles with Divorce and the Family/Financial Implications

Two years ago, Helen separated from her husband, Paul, after 12 years of marriage. They were doing well negotiating the
(continued)

coparenting agenda. Now, it was time to focus on the business aspect of divorce. During her separation, Helen became knowledgeable about their financial situation and managed her own day-to-day finances, something she had never done before. She hired a lawyer and an accountant and readied herself for dealing with the business negotiation of her divorce, a task for which she felt unqualified, knowing that Paul was a tough negotiator.

In confronting a life transition that will automatically transform a person's status from married to single, it is necessary to consider the single status and the changes that will accompany it. In transitions, although the defined result is never clear, people must take care to vet decisions through the new lens rather than the old one, since the vacillation between the old and the new reality can be confusing. In her case, Helen had to learn to think like a single person instead of a married woman.

Helen spoke to her therapist regularly about the anxiety she experienced in anticipating these negotiations. She had envisioned a much easier process. She was committed to maintaining the coparental relationship established two years ago, but affirmed her commitment to take a stance for herself, which she had never done during her marriage. She had always assumed Paul would take care of her, a premise from the past. She was challenged by the competing old and new agendas.

Transitions require shifts in premises, self-image, and action. The old and the new ideas can be contradictory, and fear of the unknown can be paralyzing. Envisioning a future can help the process. Asking, "When you picture life going forward, what do you see?" can help clients answer their fears with concrete models. Helen's ongoing conversation with her therapist helped her stay focused on how she wanted to shape her future life.

Helen's most important value related to the health of her children. She had promised herself she would not engage in a divorce battle that would have a detrimental impact on them. Her parents had warned her that she was being naïve, but she discounted this attitude, since her parents had never had any experience with these issues. She also had a sense of entitlement to what she felt to be hers, because during the past two years, she had educated herself and knew what she had the right to expect financially from her husband. She fought constantly within herself to maintain this commitment despite her natural inclination to let Paul take care of her.

Helen's therapist kept reminding her of the two elements she had chosen as her guides in this process: "relationships" and "financial responsibility." But she felt alone in this process. Every time she called her father to discuss the matter, he told her to fight for what she deserved. He focused only on the financial aspect and could never see the connection between finance and the family. Whenever she asked her father about what financial expectations she might have from him, he responded by telling her to focus on the business negotiations of her divorce. She was angry that her father was withholding information about financial planning he had done for her and her siblings. In their latest argument, they finally respectfully agreed to disagree, something they had never done before. She realized it was her responsibility to manage the tension she was feeling between her father's voice of advice, "Get as much as you can; you are entitled," and her value of maintaining her family's emotional health. She would have to compromise, but she did not yet know how.

Helen and her therapist decided to do a money/work focused genogram to further her understanding of the dilemmas she faced. In tracing these themes generationally, Helen realized that she had been raised with the assumption that she would always be taken care of by a man in her life. When she expanded what this meant vis-à-vis a worklife, this exposed yet another dimension to her dilemma. She had always been a "stay at home" mom, just as her own mother had been. Depending on the outcome of her financial settlement, Helen might have to go to work. This was counter to her mode of parenting in her own life as well as her experience growing up. She had been blind-sided to the work issue before doing this work/money focused genogram. Helen appreciated the message behind her father's statement differently. She knew that she had to spend reflective time on two specific issues: her financial responsibility and learning curve in that area and her future work life.

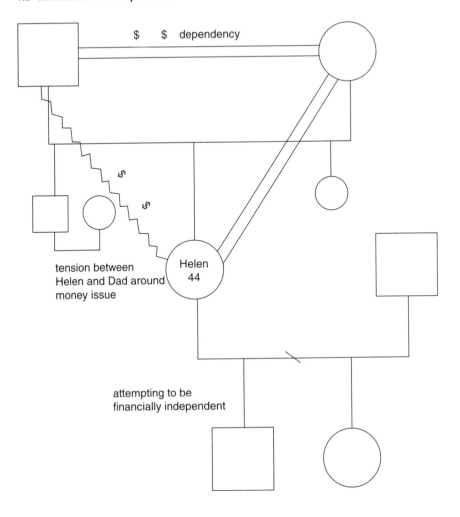

$ $ dependency

tension between
Helen and Dad around
money issue

Helen
44

attempting to be
financially independent

When the perspective of parents, friends, or confidantes differs from that of single adults, it is sometimes important to agree to disagree. As a single person, even though there might be family around, such as children and parents, one's status is still as a single adult. How single adults manage their financial and relational dimensions needs to be considered through the future single lens. In a multigenerational context, there will often be differences of opinions. It is valuable to qualify the thinking and understand the implications while developing a course of action.

Fifties, Sixties, and Older: Transformation

Case Study: Widows and Widowers Confront Their New Status

The bereavement group had been meeting for a few months. There were two men and four women ranging in age from 55 to 75. At their preceding meeting, they had decided to focus on the implications of their new single status reviewing the social, familial, and financial dimensions. Six months after her loss, Maria noted that she was just beginning to adjust to living alone day to day, while Andrew responded that it had taken him longer. They both articulated that coping with meals, sleep, and silence had required major adjustments. Both had come up with varying solutions about how to manage these issues, such as listening to music or watching TV to cover the silence, sleeping with a pillow, or making numerous dates for dinner. Jeanette chimed in with a difficulty she was having with her social status. As a couple, she and her husband were invited everywhere. Now, the invitations had stopped coming. Although she had the financial capacity to maintain her standing in the community, she was feeling rejected and was confused by it. Did it relate to gender and power?

Having been introduced to the values cards, the group began to reference these in their responses to one another. Initially, Jeanette said she felt slighted, but after one of their meetings, she worked with the card sort and started to think about what was really important to her at this stage in her life. Did she really care about those invitations or was she missing that life she had with her husband? Perhaps she was beginning to think about shaping things differently now that he was gone.

In transitioning to single status, we are called on to redefine ourselves. The complexity, especially after a partner's death, involves both mourning and redefinition. The transformation can occur by beginning to look through the lens of the single adult. In recognizing the change of status, clients can rethink how they might choose to live their life. There is no need for major adjustments. Some people try to maintain their status quo, since it can help them live with the pain of loss. Change occurs when they begin to proactively consider how to reshape life as a single person, taking into consideration the multiple dimensions of life in these middle-aged and later years. Talking about this, especially in a group where others do not have historic perceptions of the person, is a positive step toward the acceptance of a new single status.

Burt, another member of the group, raised future-oriented issues. He was thinking about how and when he could afford to retire. Where could he go with built-in recreation and socialization? How could he set up support for his future caretaking if necessary? He had determined through the card sort that finance, recreation, and relationships were top on his list. The group was surprised by his pace and practicality, but responded respectfully, acknowledging the anxiety inherent in living alone and impressed that he was already thinking ahead.

Pacing is unique to each individual. Planning for the future can reorient someone to the new reality or mask the acceptance of the change that has taken place. Both the process and its content have to be explored to understand the meaning for the client. Recognizing the coping mechanism and noting it either as part of the adjustment process or a step toward transformation is essential.

Jeanette raised a different issue that had surfaced recently. Her lawyer had suggested that she make some estate-planning decisions. He identified her as the matriarch of the family, and the term had jolted her. The decisions her lawyer was proposing required astute planning, something she and her late husband had always done together, but an art that she had not developed on her own. With whom could she consult now about familial, financial, or social issues? How could she define her new role? Would it be different from what it had been when her husband was alive? Her husband believed fervently that economics was the key to life. She did not disagree but knew and understood relationships to be significant as well. His decisions, with her knowledge, were mostly based on money as the relevant issue. She had the potential to incorporate her ideas into these decisions. Simultaneously, she noted both her fear and excitement.

She wondered how to approach the issues the lawyer had raised. The group proposed that she think about the ways she could reflect her values in her new role as matriarch. She pondered and then spontaneously responded. She wanted to celebrate her family, maintain financial independence and security, build relationships with each generation in her family, and develop her social network. That would take time and effort! How relieved she was with her response. These were the things that were most important to her as she began the next phase of her life journey as a single adult. Once she had named her values, the decisions connected to her estate became easier to think about. She could experience her resilience in anticipating the potential of her transformation.

Men and women process experiences like bereavement differently. For men, the call to action serves as protection from fear or grief. If they can *do* something, perhaps they can avoid the depth or intensity of the grief. Women are more prone to reflect and explore the new and old sets of circumstances. The combination of these two approaches to grappling with change can be empowering and therefore powerful. Jeanette, hearing Burt's action-directed plan for his retirement and his rationale for his decision making, saw him as a role model for her to consider in responding to her estate lawyer's questions. She went one step beyond Burt, applying her newly stated values and linking them to her decision making. The reworking of a values frame never gets stale. At this stage of life, it can be helpful in moving from a marital status to a single status, especially around the key financial issues that accompany this transition, including retirement, estate planning, and long-term care.

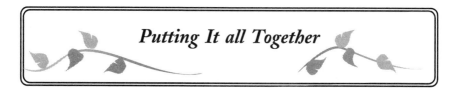

Putting It all Together

The single adult, at whatever stage of life, deals with money and financial independence. Their issues vary from initiation to financial independence to security and finally to distribution of wealth. In working with singles, the reactions to their independent financial responsibility can range from denial to obsessiveness. The particular life circumstance and the fear of the future add to the complexity. Understanding the meaning of money for single adults can expand the dimension of understanding their life experience. Using the values framework becomes an access point for expanding the view.

In Scott's situation, we see how his awareness of his mixed response to independence serves as a prime motivation for his trajectory forward. Carla comes to recognize her resistance to owning her own home based on a traditional gendered premise that no longer applies. For Helen, the focused genogram expands her understanding of the dilemmas she faces in the final steps of her divorce negotiation and the adults in the bereavement group all benefit from hearing the multiple perspectives and linkage of values as they reweave their life narratives with the collateral financial and relational implications. In each situation, the single adult develops an enhanced understanding of their values orientation and shifts their perspective.

Chapter 7

Life Transitions: Divorce, Illness, and Death

S*tress, crisis,* and *adaptation* are all words used to describe and understand how families cope with life's myriad distressing events, such as death, divorce, chronic illness, and unemployment. When such crises occur, one of the elements that is often destabilized is money. Such transitions, whether they come about abruptly or gradually, planned or spontaneously, present emotional complexities that require resilience and adaptability. It is necessary to harness both the practical and emotional components of the transition to manage crisis or change. People who have an established awareness of their values will experience greater stability as they move through the transition and its decision-making process.

The word *transition* describes a psychological process people go through to come to terms with a new life situation. Challenges and opportunities surface when changes occur in the family system. These challenges are usually embedded in roles, family structure, problem solving, and effective coping. Crisis occurs when the stress of a situation exceeds the ability of people in the family to effectively handle it. When too many stressors hit at once, the family's reservoir of coping mechanisms becomes depleted, often leading to crisis. The fewer the family's resources (including family members, friends, and financial support), the more vulnerable the family system will be. Families have different breaking points beyond which they are no longer able to cope with a critical situation. Adaptation involves finding ways to put the changes into perspective and move on with life, which can sometimes be a difficult task.

If the professional can foster a family's resilience in the face of such events, individuals and their relationships to one another can often emerge strengthened and ready to meet future life challenges. It is important for practitioners to guide their clients toward breaking the taboo of money talk in a relational context. While this might appear to be merely a practical dimension, it can contribute greatly to the stress of a transitional experience. It is critical for people experiencing stressful life events to be comfortable talking about the financial implications. Even if a client does not raise the topic, the professional has the responsibility of acknowledging the financial implications of their situation, leaving the door open for further conversation. We can accomplish this by giving clients the structure of a value system with which they can address the financial implications of these events. These interventions can alleviate some of the stress that people experience during transitions for which many are unprepared. The complexity of the landscape that forms around a crisis can become easier to navigate when there are fewer obstacles.

Awareness

Case Study: Jane's Life Changes Abruptly

Jane picked up the phone to news that would change her life forever. Her husband had just suffered a massive heart attack and was being taken to the emergency room. His condition was critical. The random thoughts in Jane's head varied from "Please let him live!" to "Why did this happen to him?" to "Will he survive?" to "Who should I call?" to "What should I do?" to "What will happen to us if he dies?"

Stan died that evening, and Jane was catapulted into a life change and transition. In 24 hours, she became a single parent responsible for raising their two children, aged 10 and 12. Besides the trauma of the death of her husband, her life partner, she had also lost the family's breadwinner. Jane had no job and no means of income. She knew that she could manage on their savings for the short term, but she also knew that she would have to make many hard practical decisions to protect her family's financial well-being. She and Stan had always said that they needed to review their financial information, but the review had always moved to the bottom of their list. She did not know where to begin. She had many competing emotions that were difficult to contain—disbelief, grief, and anxiety all converged and collided simul-taneously. Within this emotional turmoil, Jane had to address the practical issues of financial stability and raising her children. While such practical issues might seem insignificant in the face of enormous trauma and loss, Jane reasoned that addressing them might alleviate some of her anxiety.

The structure of Jane's life changed overnight. It took her years to get through the emotional aftermath of her husband's sudden death; the anxiety was like a broad band that encapsulated her family for a long time. Jane restored the family's stability when she began to master their finances and feel secure in her ability to provide for her family with full self-awareness. She had no problem keeping Stan's memory alive. She actually felt his pres-ence as she processed all the changes that were taking place for her, remembering the four things that were most important to them: education, relationships, work, and community. Remembering these shared values gave her the strength to figure out this next phase of her life. When she thought about the household budget, or her decision to work from home, or her day-to-day conversa-tions with the children, she used these values as her litmus test, making sure that her decisions and actions reflected these prio-rities. Her commitment to their values served as her connection to Stan and the memory of their life together. It became her resilience and strength.

Using values as a guide, especially during crises that bring about unanticipated change, provides a structure that gives the transition process stability. The awareness and integration of these core values into the life decisions made during these transitions bestows a security and consistency to an otherwise insecure and difficult process.

When Jane looked back on those initial months after her husband's death, she was grateful that she could make decisions according to the road map that she and Stan had set out for their life's journey together. That road map had given her the inner strength to get through such a difficult time. She was pleased with her new work from home. She could be there for her children and still make ends meet. She was glad she had joined a bereavement group at the local community center, where she found men and women who provided her with support as she managed the dilemmas that surfaced in her new life circumstances. Her fellow group members always commended her when she used her litmus test for her decisions, and her road map became a paradigm that they tried to emulate. The facilitator had been so impressed with Jane's approach that she had encouraged this reflective process for the rest of the group. It was now 18 months since her husband died, and Jane was just beginning to feel better about her life.

Implementation

Transitions can denote a significant developmental process. The pacing might vary depending on the crisis, the individual, and the family's human and financial resources. It is often helpful to think in terms of a protracted adjustment, fostering the individual and family resilience by encouraging the use of available resources.

Case Study: Lucy and Robert Plan an Important Family Meeting

Lucy had been diagnosed with multiple sclerosis many years ago. She and her husband, Robert, had adapted to the course of her disease as it had progressed. It had now become difficult for Lucy to continue to go to the office, another turning point in their lives. Their sons-in-law were both working as members of the management team of Lucy's business, where she had been grooming them for leadership, when one of their daughters decided to divorce her husband, causing Lucy a great deal of stress.

For the 45 years of their marriage, Robert had avoided talking to Lucy about her financial holdings. He had chosen to do his academic work, support the family from his salary, and let Lucy take care of their recreational and philanthropic funding. He had no idea how much money she had accumulated over the years because Lucy had a separate accountant for her business. She and her husband had not done any estate planning or discussed her succession. Robert suggested to Lucy that it might be timely, given the circumstances, for them to address certain important family business issues. Lucy knew that they would need help with these conversations,. Her own family history had been fraught with conflicts and cutoffs due to family business issues. Her strategy had been to build a defined boundary between her family life and her business life. She realized it was time to disassemble. She contacted a family business consultant who understood family dynamics as well as financial issues.

First and foremost, Lucy and Robert needed to address their financial assets and Robert needed to become more knowledgeable about Lucy's business. She had to decide about succession in her business, and they had to talk about their daughter's impending divorce, a challenge both financially and personally. In addition, as Lucy's condition worsened, they had to address some practical issues about their living conditions.

A shift in role takes place when a family faces chronic illness with either protracted or acute onset. It is not uncommon for each member of the family to take on a particular role and responsibility based on interest, skill, time, or gendered premise. Rigid role assignments, especially when they concern money, can lead to conflict when the need arises to change those roles. Managing the transition offers the opportunity to shift the roles thoughtfully and constructively.

Lucy understood the complexity of the decisions that she and Robert would be facing. They had always avoided financial discussions because she found them too painful. They had always meant facing the inevitable—the progression of her disease and its impact on their lives, the disparity of their income, the imbalance in accumulation of assets, and Robert's sensitivity to these issues. Lucy had done lots of financial planning on her own when it came to her business. But having groomed only her sons-in-law for succession, she was now confronting the flaw in her thought process, and she realized that she had to bring Robert and her daughters into her business world as well. She had to break the taboo around money talk because they needed to make decisions together before she moved into the next stages of her disease.

The challenge for the professional confronted with these complex circumstances is to facilitate a conversation that acknowledges the emotional component of the situation and also addresses its practical issues. The intersection of multiple systems at play can be overwhelming. Distinguishing between fact and emotion while discerning the issues and nuances among the multiple perspectives can be challenging. For the professional, using the values clarification exercise as an organizing construct provides a stable platform with which to move in and out of the various systems, defining the issues within each area and clarifying the meanings.

The consultant suggested that Robert and Lucy come to see her alone for the initial meeting to begin the process of assessment and clarification. Robert provided the medical history and prognosis. Lucy gave the financial picture and the corporate structure, and both of them constructed the family's genogram.

They placed much data on the table. The challenge for the consultant was to create the safe environment within which a discussion of the complexities could ensue. The consultant decided to use the values clarification exercises as a point of departure, even though Robert and Lucy bridled initially when she presented the idea. The consultant explained that since they would be making many decisions during the next few months, it would be extremely helpful to know which values would be guiding them. She expected to use these values as a foundation, noting that this would give them a frame of reference for their discussions, especially when they were ready to bring in their daughters.

Using both sets of cards for clarification, the consultant discovered that there was definitely common ground between Robert and Lucy on the content values. The point of departure came with their process

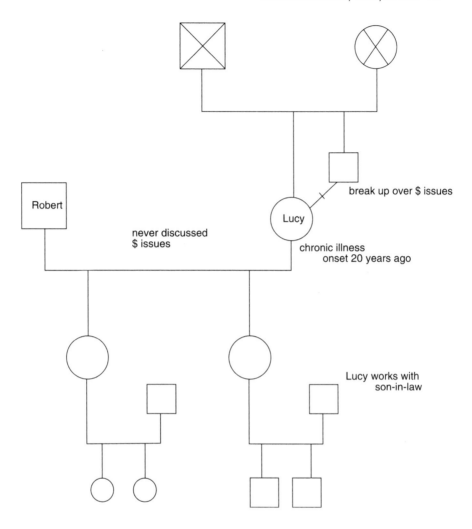

values, which reflected that they had avoided making joint decisions throughout their marriage. The consultant, realizing that this would become their stumbling block, ended their session suggesting postponement of the upcoming scheduled family meeting.

The pacing and sequencing of bringing family members together for a family meeting can be significant. The more complex the issues, the more families need to establish clarification before facilitating the conversation with multiple generations. This family had complex medical, financial, and familial issues to discuss. The consultant needed to understand how much information had been shared with whom, as it related to health, finance, and family. Robert and Lucy had never used the format of a family meeting for any previous conversations. Their pattern had been to schedule one-on-one conversations with individual family members. The ultimate goal now was to have a family meeting that included their daughters, where Lucy and Robert would describe the estate planning they were doing as well as the rationale behind their decision making. They would include their thinking about what the future would bring from a medical, financial, and familial perspective.

Robert's reaction to this first meeting was mixed. Although he experienced the consultant as knowledgeable, empathic, and focused, he had his doubts about the values approach that she was proposing. He agreed to go along with it, but was skeptical about its effectiveness. Lucy, however, was impressed with the approach and saw merit in using values as their organizing principles. She had actually applied some of the issues at hand to this approach. Because of the upcoming divorce, she was not sure about including the sons-in-law in the conversation. By restricting the conversation to her daughters, she left it up to them to decide whether to share the information with their respective husbands. She decided to discuss the business plan separately with the divorcing son-in-law, a format the consultant had suggested as a way of creating varying boundaries for managing the tension between inclusiveness and exclusivity. Lucy, using "transparency," "empowerment," and "dialogue" as her principles, liked the plan. Robert was more hesitant and needed to consider it further, because of the gravity of the three parallel transitions; their daughter's divorce, shifting leadership in the business, and Lucy's adjustment to this next phase of her life.

Integrating values into the decision-making process demands reflective thought to explore the options and implications, since tensions often surface. When this happens, the consultant or therapist must ensure that the client understands the decision will come as a result of engagement in the process. The creation of boundaries for these discussions provides the element of safety for clients, while the focus on implementation leads to resolution over time.

Robert, Lucy, and their consultant had all prepared material for the next session. At their second meeting, they reviewed the list of issues that needed resolution to reach their objective of preparedness for a family meeting. The consultant had met with the daughters and now had a better handle on their perspectives for the transitions that were taking place.

Lucy had provided the business lists, and Robert had done more research on the medical issues they might have to confront. They narrowed the list of issues to the most significant ones. The consultant then facilitated the conversation by having them integrate their values into the discussion as an added dimension. Robert was amazed by the personal accessibility of the conversation. He could distinguish for himself and Lucy where his emotional reactions and their values intersected to cause the inherent confusion that had blocked them in the past. Never before had they reached this level of discussion. Although they did not agree on many issues, for the first time in years they had a constructive conversation about financial decisions. By the time they left this meeting, they had addressed the majority of the issues on their list.

The consultant was amazed by their progress. This was the first time she had broached these issues in this way, and she found that the new tools she had used had given her a greater sense of meaning in her work.

Transformation

The integration of values into the decision-making process provides a significant structure for both the professional and the family. The challenge comes in managing the tensions that unfold when applying these values to decision making. Competing issues may arise with the complexity of the particular client's issues. When the conversation shifts from finding solutions to managing the dilemmas, a values-based approach generates greater accessibility to decision making.

Case Study: Paul Reshapes Life at Retirement

Paul, a 50-year-old single man, had worked for over 20 years in the cosmetic industry. He had been the creative director in a division he had helped to develop from its inception, but it

(continued)

was now time for him to move on. He was presently living in a significant but fairly new relationship with Charles. His parents, who lived on the West Coast, were aging, and he was planning to move them east. Anxious about his employment status, he decided to look for fulfilling volunteer work. Paul was looking forward to a more meaningful life. He was concerned about how he would manage the financial, work, and family issues that these changes would bring about, and so he decided to return to his old therapist to sort out the competing internal and external shifts that were about to take place.

Life changes can be the result of external as well as internal forces. The convergence of these forces may cause disruption and feelings of dislocation. Sorting out the change requires action, reflective thinking, and connection to one's emotional process. The lack of normal structure can be replaced with an internal compass gained through awareness and the definition of values.

We all have multiple roles or identities that inform who we are and how we behave. The consistency of our core values, however, is manifest in our inner compass despite the many roles we play. The ability to contextualize the meaning of these values as we transition through stressful events and reassign their relevance becomes the challenge in times of transformation.

Paul was about to change his entire life and was naturally apprehensive. His therapist reviewed his motivations for making these changes and found that Paul needed to identify the values that provided meaning to this shift. He knew that family relationships were important to him and understood that his parents were aging and needed more attention from him. He was also ready now to do more work in the not-for-profit sector, beginning to volunteer his services, something he had wanted to do for a long time. His concern was the financial dimension, and whether he could afford to do all this. Since Paul's anxiety surfaced every time he talked about this, the therapist needed to understand what the reality was, and so she began a fact-finding conversation about Paul's financial situation.

The question of how far to probe into someone's financial life is a touchy subject for many therapists. But in the same way that a professional might explore the details of someone's sexual life, gentle probing into financial matters can be vitally important. Often, the client has not aligned reality and anxiety around money, and only thorough exploration can detect that discrepancy. A therapist's reluctance to address money issues impedes this process.

Paul was keenly aware of the values that had informed his decision to change his life, and thus could curb his anxiety with the conversations about his financial situation. At monthly check-ins with his therapist, he reported the success of his transition. He had cut back on dinners in fancy restaurants, and Charles was contributing more to household expenses. His parents were comfortably settled near him, and he was living the life he wanted to live. The smooth transition astounded him. He had anticipated so much anxiety, and in the end none had occurred. He assigned that success to the full conversations and clarity of values with which he had made the transition. He had transformed his lifestyle in a way that truly reflected his values of family and community, with financial responsibility as an underlying force instead of the front runner.

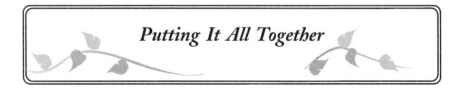

Putting It All Together

Each vignette presented in this chapter illustrates a transition for the members of a family. Movement through a transition cannot always be controlled or managed, due to life's unpredictable circumstances. What helps in each case is a values paradigm for decision making. When we consider Jane's traumatic loss and her resilience, we see how she used a values map to guide her through the real-life decisions she confronts. Although, as seen in Chapter 6, Helen's circumstances are completely different, she too determines the key values that will inform her decision making as she negotiates her business divorce For Lucy, the application of process values helps her identify her dilemmas and resolve them discretely. In these case studies, money is a key factor. The linkage of values to money provides the lens for decision making and informs the resolution beyond the financial implications.

Money can be the central issue or, as in Paul's case, the layer that has to be addressed to expand and enjoy life more fully. The ability to address the money theme in all these life situations is central to helping clients in their decision making. If the professional can facilitate these conversations and not shy away from the subject, those clients will be better served.

Conclusion

Money infuses all aspects of our lives. It is a crucial practical element to which we attach multiple emotional meanings. Even so, money has remained an underexplored issue in our professional world for too long. Significant conversations seldom occur between professionals and clients, among family members, or in our internal dialogue. The tools described in this book are keys to open the door to conversations that explore money's multiple meanings from practical, psychological, and philosophical perspectives. The applications we have described reflect the potential uses of these tools. In deciding which of the many possible ways to use them, the professional should always consider the objectives of the conversations, the specific life circumstances of the client, and other accompanying issues.

How to Use These Tools

The tools highlighted in this book can be useful in various ways and in different settings: one-on-one conversations, work with couples, family work, family meetings, group seminars, and group meetings. The cards become a structure and stimulant for conversations about values and money. The focused genogram enables going beyond the issue at hand to explore how the past has informed the present. Some of my colleagues have used the card sort as an entry point to the family of origin influence by asking clients to differentiate their parents' values from their own. Many users have begun applying these approaches in one setting and eventually expanded them to others as they see ways that different people can benefit from these conversations.

Both professionals and their clients use the tools to go beyond surface issues and access the underlying contradictions. Thus, Charles, preparing for a family meeting with his sons, first used the cards to *identify contradictions* in his life, and the normalization of these discrepancies helped clarify his conversation with his sons. In other cases, these tools may help *clarify a discrepancy* in people's process of financial decision making. Art and Yvonne, whose conversations about retirement planning could not proceed until they had a *new understanding* about their respective relationships to financial decision making, used the tools this way with their counselor. Finally, the card sort structures a *format for a group discussion* to explore the multiple perspectives so often found in families. A group setting allowed different perspectives to surface in the case of Harold, who could understand the practice of collaboration with his adult children after Jane, another member of his group, explained it to him.

Incorporating this approach into the professional's toolbox can help clinicians or counseling professionals discover their own tensions around money. They will be motivated to learn more about their attitudes to money and will explore with greater depth the premises that inform them. What professionals can learn from this approach can advance their understanding of themselves and their skills in facilitation.

These tools also help professionals support clients directly in the following ways:

- Create safety and provide positive language for facilitating money conversations.
- Connect the content and the process of future sessions.
- Aid in the pacing and sequencing of money conversations.
- Provide entrée to a subject that has been taboo for too long.

Moreover, bringing money and values together in conversation for clients can have many freeing and transformative effects in their lives and relationships. Introducing this approach to clients immediately raises their consciousness of values in their lives. The case of David and Olivia, whose budgeting disagreements stemmed from different ways of expressing some overlapping values, illustrates how defining values can neutralize the tension and activate a new direction for the money conversation. For couples and families, providing access to the meaning of money can begin the transformative process.

The content and process values cards can help clients address the "how" of making and implementing decisions. The card sorts provide meaning and personal agency for clients, empowering them in their decision making and bringing about reflective thought in the following areas:

- Enhance a family's capacity to have constructive conversations.
- Serve as an ongoing paradigm for present and future conversations with or without a facilitator.
- Increase family resilience and strengthen family ties.

In essence, these tools are open-ended. Anytime we want to support awareness and transformation of values about money or indeed about any other source of tension, this approach can give us options for doing so.

Epilogue

Throughout the past three decades of my career as a family systems thinker and practitioner, in both the clinical and consultative space, I have been privileged to be at the cusp of explorations that have provoked thought, engendered sensitivity, and promoted self-awareness. Embedded in this book are two new ideas that I hope will stimulate more conversations among our professional community. The first idea references the promotion of values. The second is the anticipation that opening the conversation about money with and among ourselves and our clients will lead to exploring the ever-present class issues within our society.

Promoting values walks the line between maintaining a clinician's neutrality and promoting the conversation about meaning for people. Promoting the consciousness of a value system is a new idea in our field of practice. The paradigm urges a *consciousness of values* rather than a specific set of values. In this practice, there is space to consider behavior, insight, social context, discrepancy, and clarity. In creating the linkage between money and values, we trigger people's reflective thought process about the meaning of money and the place of values in their lives. The linkage promotes a values discussion for families, which has long been a no-go area, and it stimulates all of us to seek more meaning in our lives while empowering us to find it. These conversations will naturally lead professionals to be reflective about their values and will require them to assess their influence on the context.

Although many of us share universal values such as humanity, freedom, and the pursuit of happiness, we rarely talk about what these mean in practice and where and how we reconcile the differences between our ideals and our daily actions. This methodology, attending to content and process, highlights that very discrepancy. It forces the unpacking of inherent contradictions, and confronts the convergence and divergence of values when applied to specific circumstances. It raises choices and meaning for clients within a relational context. It pushes us to look at our understanding and perspective of these issues.

If we unpack major issues and look at common discrepancies in our societal context, we may stimulate the discussion of class. To date, our field has pushed toward further exploration of gender and race. In each area, there is attention to power, privilege, and social justice, all components of interpersonal behavior and social context. When we started talking about sex, we began to talk about gender. More recently, when we started talking about violence, the conversation evolved to issues of social justice. I hope that the ideas in this book will serve as a catalyst to this other unspoken subject that shadows our societal and relational context. Perhaps allowing people to talk about money will inspire them to talk about class, a subject that has never been thoroughly explored in the realm of psychotherapy. The definition of class historically has related to education and economics. The inclusion and consciousness of both content and process values might serve to expand that definition.

This methodology promotes an ongoing dynamic process that individuals and families can internalize and use as a system of checks and balances, both individually and interpersonally. Following the continuum from decision making to self-determination to responsibility can enhance that continuum and develop more responsible people in families and communities. It will force people to be more accountable with each other. It will give a deeper meaning to their lives and generate a force for good.

Bibliography

1. Bowen, Murray. *Family Therapy in Clinical Practice.* New York: Jason Aronson, 1978.
2. Carter, Betty, and Monica McGoldrick, eds. *The Expanded Family Life Cycle: Individual, Family and Social Perspectives.* Boston: Allyn and Bacon, 1999.
3. Fithian, S. C. *Values-Based Estate Planning.* New York: John Wiley & Sons, 2000.
4. Gersick, Kelin E., John A. Davis, Marion McCollom Hampton, and Ivan Landsberg. *Generation to Generation: Life Cycles of the Family Business.* Boston, MA: Harvard Business School Press, 1997.
5. Godfrey, Joline. *Raising Financially Fit Kids.* Berkeley, Toronto, Canada: Ten Speed Press, 2003.
6. Hughes, Jr., James E. *Family Wealth: Keeping It in the Family.* Revised and Expanded ed. Princeton, NJ: Bloomberg Press, 2004.
7. Hughes, Jr., James E. *Family: The Compact among Generations.* New York: Bloomberg Press, 2007.
8. Levinson, Daniel J. *The Season's of a Man's Life.* New York: Ballantine Books, 1978.
9. Madanes, Cloe, with Claudio Madanes. *The Secret Meaning of Money: How It Binds Together Families in Love, Envy, Compassion, or Anger.* San Francisco: Jossey-Bass, 1994.
10. McGoldrick, Monica, and Randy Gerson. *Genograms in Family Assessment.* New York: W.W. Norton, 1985.

11. Mogel, Wendy. *The Blessing of a Skinned Knee: Using Jewish Teachings to Raise Self-Reliant Children*. New York: Penguin Compass, 2001.
12. Peck, Judith Stern."A Room of One's Own . . . and 500 Pounds." *Journal of Feminist Family Therapy* (Winter, 1992).
13. Peck, Judith Stern. *"Families Launching Young Adults."* In *Reweaving the Family Tapestry: A Multigenerational Approach to Families*, edited by Fredda Herz Brown. New York: W.W. Norton, 1991.
14. Peck, Judith Stern, and Fredda Herz Brown, "Families in the Divorce and Post Divorce Process." In *Reweaving the Family Tapestry: A Mulitgenerational Approach to Families*, edited by Fredda Herz Brown. New York: W.W. Norton, 1991.
15. Peck, Judith Stern, and Jennifer Manocherian "Divorce in the Changing Family Life Cycle." In *The Changing Family Life Cycle*, edited by Betty Carter and Monica McGoldrick. John Wiley & Sons, Inc., 1980.
16. Schervish, Paul G. "The Moral Biography of Wealth: Philosophical Reflections on the Foundation of Philanthropy." *Nonprofit and Voluntary Sector Quarterly* (September 2006): 477–492.
17. Schervish, Paul G., Cathlene Williams, and Lilya Wagner. "The Inheritance of Wealth and the Commonwealth: The Ideal of Paideia in an Age of Affluence." In *Philanthropy across the Generations: New Directions for Philanthropic Fundraising*, edited by Dwight F. Burlingame, (Winter, 2003): 5–24.
18. Shapiro, Margaret. "Money: A Therapeutic Tool for Couples." Family Process (September 2007): 279–292.
19. Sheinberg, Marcia, and Ackerman Faculty. *The Ackerman Institute's Relational Approach to Family Therapy*. 2003.
20. Steiger, Heidi L., ed. *Wealthy and Wise: Secrets about Money*. Hoboken, NJ: John Wiley & Sons, Inc., 2003.

Appendix I

Content Values Cards

These cards are also available online at www.wiley.com/go/money andmeaning.

Personal Values

- Modesty
- Loyalty
- Faithfulness

© 2004 Ackerman Institute

Economic Values

- Financial responsibility
- Maximizing profit
- Frugality

© 2004 Ackerman Institute

Ethical Values

- Integrity
- Justice
- Fairness

Philanthropic Values

- Contribution of time
- And money
- To care for others

Financial Values

- Financial independence
- Preservation of wealth
- Stewardship

Public Values

- Good citizenship
- Community involvement
- Government service

Physical Values

- Health
- Relaxation
- Quiet time alone
- Exercise

Spiritual Values

- Inner spirituality
- Faith
- Religious commitments

Relational Values

- Family
- Friends
- Work associates

Cultural Values

- Music
- Visual arts
- Travel

Work Values

- Professional achievement
- Competence
- Stewardship

Educational Values

- Study
- Self-improvement
- Academic achievement

Recreational Values

- Sports
- Leisure activity
- Hobbies
- Family vacations

Material Values

- Possessions
- Life style
- Social standing

Appendix II

Process Values Cards

These cards are also available online at www.wiley.com/go/money andmeaning.

Collaboration

Do we make decisions jointly?

Exclusivity

Do we exclude certain family members from making decisions based on age, bloodline, gender, or other issues?

Dialogue

Do we encourage discussion and are we open to hearing each other as we make decisions?

Equality

Do we make decisions using equality as our principle, treating everyone the same?

Reflective Thinking

Are we contemplative in our approach, gathering information and exploring as we make decisions?

Transparency

Do we disclose relevant information and our rationales as we make decisions?

Hierarchy

Are decisions made in an autocratic way with one individual in a dominant position?

Inclusivity

Do we include all family members in our decision making?

Empowerment

Do we authorize other family members to make decisions?

Index